ENGLISH PROVERBS
EXPLAINED

English Proverbs Explained

by

RONALD RIDOUT

and

CLIFFORD WITTING

HEINEMANN

LONDON

Heinemann Educational Books Ltd
LONDON EDINBURGH MELBOURNE AUCKLAND TORONTO
HONG KONG SINGAPORE KUALA LUMPUR NEW DELHI
IBADAN NAIROBI LUSAKA JOHANNESBURG
KINGSTON

ISBN 0 435 10751 8

First published 1967
© Ronald Ridout and Clifford Witting 1967
Reprinted 1968, 1974, 1977

Published by
Heinemann Educational Books Ltd
48 Charles Street, London W1X 8AH
Printed Offset Litho and bound in Great Britain by
Cox & Wyman Ltd, London, Fakenham and Reading

Contents

Introduction   1

Alphabetical List of Proverbs
    with Explanations   15

Biographical Details   175

Index   178

Introduction

This is a collection of English proverbs still in current use. We have arranged them in alphabetical order (ignoring only *A, An* and *The*) to make for ease of reference, and we have explained them and illustrated them straightforwardly to make for ease of reading. For those who are not sure of the proverb they wish to look up, or who know a slightly different version of it, we have added an exhaustive index of prominent words, so that almost any proverb may be readily tracked down by its number.

Which proverbs are still in use and which have gone out of use is inevitably a matter of personal judgement. In any case a proverb may have disappeared in one part of the English-speaking world and yet be very much alive in another. Then within a single country a certain proverb may still be in use among rural people though it has completely disappeared from the cities. We have therefore erred on the generous side and included eight hundred proverbs rather than the five or six hundred to which the list of current proverbs is sometimes reduced. Even if some of them are beginning to sound a little old-fashioned, the reader is likely to come across them in his reading and may therefore need to look them up.

It should be abundantly clear that we have written this book with the general reader in mind rather than the man of letters. We have been concerned with proverbs as a live force in spoken and written English of recent times, not with proverbs as an academic or historical study. We hope that in addition to the general reader at home the book will be specially useful to the many students and users of English as a foreign language.

What are proverbs?

The definition of a proverb given in *The Advanced Learner's Dictionary of Current English* is as good as any: a 'popular short saying, with words of advice or warning'. Yet it is far from enabling us to identify a proverb with any certainty. Is any widely used short saying a proverb? The important word seems to be 'popular'. But how popular must a saying be to become a proverb? The line must evidently be drawn somewhere. We suggest that in the real sense of the word it must be thoroughly 'of the people'. It follows from this that it will usually be an old saying, since it is unlikely to become part of the popular consciousness in a short period of time. There are of course exceptions, and some proverbs jump into the popular mind with unusual rapidity, though we should have to exclude the purely transient catch-phrases like 'I couldn't care less' or 'What's the odds?'

The definition might have said 'a short wise saying', but presumably this was thought unnecessary as the word 'saying', when used in this way, implies wisdom. For wisdom is the other main ingredient of the proverb. To become popular it must at least appear outstandingly wise; to remain popular it must in truth contain enduring wisdom. That having been said, however, the fact remains that some wise sayings have become proverbs, while others equally wise have not; they have been lost or they have remained merely occasional quotations. It is impossible to account fully for this, but part of the reason certainly has to do with succinctness. The sayings that have won readiest acceptance have in general been the most pithy. Because they have been short, to the point, packed full, and neat in form, they have gained quick and lasting entry to the public mind. Other things being equal, the long-winded, the over-fussy, the formless saying hàs had little chance of making the grade.

It is these positive qualities that make the saying memorable, and by its very nature a proverb is memorable. The devices used in their expression to support this memorable quality are worth noting. Rhyme and assonance are one such device, e.g.:

Little strokes fell great oaks, 419
Cast ne'er a clout till May is out, 70
There's many a slip 'twixt the cup and the lip, 655
A stitch in time saves nine, 619

A simple balanced form is perhaps the commonest device of all, e.g.:

More haste, less speed, 470
Like father, like son, 409
Easy come, easy go, 160
Two is company, three is none, 703

Brevity is of course an essential aspect of memorable sayings. There are very few proverbs that are at all long, and many of the most popular ones are very short indeed, e.g.:

Boys will be boys, 59
Dead men tell no tales, 104
Every dog has his day, 173
Never say die, 492
Better late than never, 48
Let sleeping dogs lie, 397
Forewarned is forearmed, 222
What must be must be, 736
Practice makes perfect, 562
The bait hides the hook, 31

Origins

To become a proverb, a saying has to be taken up and assimilated by the common people. In the process, its origin is forgotten. Once it has become proverbial, the saying is used as part of popular wisdom; the user is no longer interested in its origin. It is safe to assume that every proverb had an origin in a specific person or specific situation, but with many of the very old ones this origin has been completely lost. It is therefore legitimate and convenient to say that proverbs have a popular origin; that they have their source in the collective wisdom of the people. In many cases this must have been as nearly literally true as makes no odds. In the numerous proverbs that summarize everyday experience, the saying probably did grow gradually into its proverbial form without any one single originator. *Make hay while the sun shines* (436), with its origin in farm work, is a case in point. Every farm worker would have felt the truth of this thought without perhaps putting it into quite those words. But after a great many people had expressed the thought in their many different ways, and by trial and error it had at last found its most memorable form, it was in that form that it lived on as a proverb. In the same way, *Don't put all your eggs in one basket* (140) would have developed out of the common-sense experience of produce marketing.

On the other hand, it is equally evident that many other proverbs have had their origin in a specific wise man. If it was in a wise man of oral tradition, we shall of course have no recorded evidence, but if it was in a wise man whose thoughts were written down, we can sometimes trace the source. In general we can assume that proverbs with the more abstract type of wisdom began life in this way, proverbs like *The end justifies the means* (164), which appears to have taken its bow in a seventeenth-century theological treatise, or *The wish is father to the thought* (768), which as far as we know was first given expression to by Julius Caesar, or *A soft answer turneth away wrath* (605), which certainly took that precise form from the Bible.

Yet who is to say that these proverbs weren't already part of the oral tradition long before they made their first appearance in print? Proverbs were at their height in Shakespeare's time, and it is more than probable that any proverb attributable to Shakespeare had a previous existence, even if in a less memorable form. It is the same with the Bible. Its proverbial wisdom is almost certainly not original. The scribes gave enduring form to wisdom that was already part of the Hebrew oral tradition. That form in turn was given an English form by the scribes of the Authorized Version.

The farther we push back our inquiry, the deeper most proverbs become lost in the lives of bygone people. Even when we take a source in a relatively modern writer like Milton, can anyone believe that his *They also serve who only stand and wait* (672) hadn't also been a wise thought in the minds of many people before him? He gave it the final enduring form, but he was working with familiar thoughts, since *There is nothing new under the sun* (668).

In any case, the two sources, the obviously popular and the apparently literary, increasingly mingled. With the spread of the printed word, sayings of wise men percolated down all the faster to the common people, who, if they found them to their liking, turned them into proverbs. Contrariwise, snatches of popular common sense readily found their way, often under disguise, into the writings of wise men.

Borrowings

Another important source of English proverbs is those of other languages. Here again it is difficult to be certain. If a proverb existed in Latin, French or Spanish before it appeared in English, there is no proof that it was borrowed from the other language. It may very well be that it developed concurrently in English but happened never to have been recorded. After all, wisdom over a whole range of subjects is common to all countries. Even when it is evident that it was genuinely borrowed from another language, as is the case with a good many of classical origin, we are still far from the ultimate source of the proverb. A Latin proverb found in this or that Latin author may not have been of his own invention any more than those of English authors, for the history of proverbs in ancient Rome or Greece must have been much the same as in England, and many wise sayings in literature owed much or all of their existence to a popular oral tradition.

Some of our borrowed proverbs have been thoroughly assimilated, but it is remarkable how many have not. We do not have to remember the Latin proverb to recognize as a proverb *He gives twice who gives quickly* (267); but the proverb *Through hardship to the stars* (682) sounds alien and less of a proverb than the Latin *Per ardua ad astra*. A number of borrowed proverbs have remained more common in their original form than in translation. Among them are:

Cherchez la femme, 80
Honi soit qui mal y pense, 310
Noblesse oblige, 509
In vino veritas, 345
Verb. sap., 709
Caveat emptor, 77

Biblical proverbs

Proverbs deriving from the Bible are in a sense another kind of borrowing, since the Bible is a translation from the Hebrew, and its wise sayings were Hebrew wisdom. Those of them that were entirely original, and they can have been but few, owed something at least to a Hebrew oral tradition; but the majority were directly from the Hebrew people or were close reflections of their traditional wisdom.

In earlier times the English Bible was so widely read that many of its sayings have become so much part of popular wisdom that few users today are aware of their biblical origin, and the hardiest free-thinker will show no hesitation in drawing upon them to illustrate a rational point. Nevertheless, a good many English proverbs come straight from the Authorized Version, e.g.:

You cannot serve God and mammon, 790
The spirit is willing, but the flesh is weak, 614
The labourer is worthy of his hire, 384
A soft answer turneth away wrath, 605

Many more are closely derivative though their wording has changed, e.g.:

Sow the wind and reap the whirlwind, 608
Spare the rod and spoil the child, 609
You cannot make bricks without straw, 786

Other literary sources

Next to the Bible, Shakespeare is undoubtedly the greatest literary source of the modern proverb. No one can be sure, however, which of those attributed to him are the product of Shakespeare's own thought and how many were taken over more or less in the form in which they existed in the oral tradition around him. Scholars are still bringing to light proverbs, long since defunct, embedded in Shakespearian lines that have been supposed pure Shakespeare. A number of proverbs from Shakespeare have survived in their original wording, e.g.:

Brevity is the soul of wit, 61
Sweet are the uses of adversity, 629
Cowards die many times before their deaths, 95

Others are adaptations from a quotation from Shakespeare, e.g.:

A rose by any other name would smell as sweet, 589

Of the many other literary sources, here is a selection:

Gather ye rosebuds while ye may (Herrick), 229
A little learning is a dangerous thing (Pope), 417
Blessed is he who expects nothing, for he shall never be disappointed (Pope), 56
Where ignorance is bliss, 'tis folly to be wise (Gray), 754
A thing of beauty is a joy for ever (Keats), 675

Household words

In trying to gain a clear understanding of the nature of the proverb it is useful to think of a half-way house between a common quotation and a true proverb, in which the quotation becomes a household word. Thus at some point a quotation from Shakespeare, like 'Cowards die many times before their deaths', acquires such wide currency that many of the people who use it cease to know where it comes from. When this happens it has already begun to lose some of its characteristic as a quotation and to take on some of the characteristic of a popular saying. It has temporarily become a part of the consciousness of the common people. If it remains there long enough and maintains its currency, it will eventually join the ranks of established proverbs. In the case of 'Cowards die many times before their deaths', we consider this has in fact occurred. Only a few people who happen to be familiar with their Shakespeare have any idea of where the proverb comes from and yet it has wide currency among all classes of people, largely, no doubt, because of its very succinct expression of a significant thought with almost universal application.

Shakespeare has been much read, especially in the last century or so, and many Shakespearian quotations have become household words at one time or another, and many still are household words, and yet not all have become proverbs. What appears to happen is that these quotations reach a certain stage of popularity but progress no farther. They may linger on for many years in much the same state of popularity, or they may fall back into the ranks of pure quotation, but in neither case do they finally make the grade of proverbs. But which do make the grade and which do not must clearly be to some extent a matter of personal judgement. For example, another popular quotation from *Cymbeline*, 'Golden lads and girls all must, as chimney-sweepers, come to dust', has in some books been listed as a proverb, whereas the present compilers feel that, as a line has to be drawn somewhere, this one has not made the grade and remains no more than a household saying, perhaps because it smacks a little too much of the literary to lie quite comfortably on the popular tongue.

Other quotations which have from time to time been listed as proverbs, but which we feel more rightly belong to this half-way stage of household words, include the following:

Even the weariest river winds somewhere safe to sea (Swinburne)
God's in his heaven – All's right with the world! (Browning)
Full many a flower is born to blush unseen (Gray)
The best is yet to be (Browning)
The wages of sin is death (Romans)
The wind bloweth where it listeth (John)
Render therefore unto Caesar the things which are Caesar's; and
   unto God the things that are God's (Matthew)

Reading maketh a full man, conference a ready man, writing an
   exact man (Bacon)
There is a divinity that shapes our ends, rough-hew them how we
   may (Shakespeare)
Frailty, thy name is woman! (Shakespeare)
No man but a blockhead ever wrote except for money (Samuel
   Johnson)

It can be seen therefore that proverbs are fluid and in a constant
state of flux. We go on adding and subtracting. Wholly new ones
from modern democratic and industrial times are finding a place too.
We have, for example, listed:

There are wheels within wheels, 648
There are two sides to every question, 647
No man is indispensable, 505
Don't speak to the man at the wheel, 145

If we had drawn the line a little lower we might also have added:

Power tends to corrupt, and absolute power corrupts absolutely
There are three kinds of lies: lies, damned lies, and statistics
You can fool some of the people all the time, and all of the people
   some of the time; but you can't fool all of the people all the time

Proverbial expressions

Certain highly idiomatic phrases in constant use, sometimes referred
to as proverbial expressions, must be distinguished from true proverbs. *To cry for the moon*, meaning to ask for the impossible, is one
such expression. On its own it offers no advice and gives no warning;
it is not a proverb. However, it can very easily be turned into a
proverb by incorporating it in the form of advice, e.g. *Don't cry for
the moon* or *Only fools cry for the moon.*
   There are many hundreds of these idiomatic phrases and most of
them can be turned into proverbs without much difficulty, and at
some time or another most of them have been so treated. This causes
confusion. Are the results proverbs or not? Again it is a matter of
personal judgement. If they are used as proverbs often enough, it
seems to us that they must be allowed to rank as proverbs, and we
have in fact listed a number of the commonest, e.g.:

to be out of the wood: Do not halloo till you are out of the wood, 131

a snake in the grass: Take heed of the snake in the grass, 632

a skeleton in the cupboard: Every family has a skeleton in the cupboard, 174

to put the cart before the horse: Don't put the cart before the horse, 142

to ride the high horse: Don't ride the high horse, 144

to tell tales out of school: Don't tell tales out of school, 148

Many others nearly as common could have been turned into proverbs, but we have not listed them, since the line had to be drawn somewhere. Examples are:

to make a virtue of necessity: Don't make a virtue of necessity

to know which side your bread is buttered on: You must know which side your bread is buttered on

to set one's house in order: One should set one's own house in order first

to have two strings to one's bow: It is wise to have two strings to one's bow

to know how many beans make five: He who knows how many beans make five is not to be cheated

to kill two birds with one stone: Who kills two birds with one stone is twice rewarded

to jump out of the frying-pan into the fire: It is a luckless fish that leaps from the frying-pan into the fire

Interpretation

How are proverbs to be interpreted? What is their full meaning? This is clearly bound up with their use and goes right to the heart of the problem. The Dutch call proverbs the daughters of experience, and we have seen how many of the oldest ones were originally a summary of what experience had taught people in the performance of everyday chores. They were, then, at the outset interpreted literally. *A stitch in time saves nine* (619) was the literal truth the busy housewife had learnt in looking after her family's clothes. It is still sound advice often given in this sense today. But as a proverb its existence depends on its ability to be applied metaphorically to a wide range of other activities, till its essential meaning has nothing to do with mending clothes, but becomes a warning that if something goes wrong you should attend to it at once, because if you don't it will be much more difficult to put right later on.

The same can be said of *Too many cooks spoil the broth* (695). It is still literally good advice, but the saying would not have survived as a proverb if it had not taken on wider metaphorical application. We do not have to look far to realize that many of the commonest proverbs are in this class, e.g.:

Don't count your chickens before they are hatched, 124
A bird in the hand is worth two in the bush, 52
The proof of the pudding is in the eating, 569
A burnt child dreads the fire, 65
Hunger is the best sauce, 315

It is difficult to believe that any of these sayings would have attained proverbial status in their literal sense. Indeed their extension by metaphorical application to other situations must have occurred early in their history. It is rarely till they have acquired this wider application that they are brought to our notice at all in the recorded evidence.

How were these sayings given their wider application? It has been suggested that they had to wait for the literary mind to show the way. But to think this is to misunderstand the genius of language as used by the common people. We see no reason to suppose that the common people would not in the course of their handling of such sayings give them other applications and so gradually build up their metaphorical quality. At the same time, an individual proverb may well have been set off on its metaphorical course by being quoted with a transferred meaning to give point to some other subject a writer was dealing with.

There are, however, very many proverbs that will not fit into this class of sayings that depend on their metaphorical application for their essential meaning. What other application, except of the little joke of applying it to grown men, is there for a proverb like *Boys will be boys* (59)? Other proverbs that are intended more or less literally include these well-known ones:

If at first you don't succeed, try, try, try again, 320
Dying is as natural as living, 155
Do as you would be done by, 121

What must be must be, 736
Waste not, want not, 715
Practise what you preach, 563
You never know what you can do till you try, 796

These and many more have survived as proverbs in spite of not needing the kind of metaphorical application that gives other proverbs their essential quality. Possibly the explanation is that these already contain a generalized truth and therefore have no need of a non-literal application to take on the generalized quality that is perhaps the ultimate characteristic of the proverbial saying.

It must be added that the more sophisticated proverbs that come to us from literature make their first appearance fully developed. They do not have to go through a literal phase at all. Perhaps they had gone through such a phase, though, before they came out of the end of the writer's pen. At all events, such proverbs as *A soft answer turneth away wrath* (605) and *Brevity is the soul of wit* (61) appear to have arrived fully developed.

The proverb in education

The proverb has had a long and honourable history in the class-room. As early as the tenth century proverbs were used in England as a brighter method of teaching Latin. Many generations of children through the nineteenth century and beyond were expected to improve their minds as well as their writing by having to copy proverbs out in their copy-books. The commonest proverbs still form part of the background of every English-speaking child, and this is recognized in the early stages of modern education, where many and varied uses are made of them. There is hardly an English course that does not somewhere draw help from them. Because of the generalized nature of proverbs, they can be used up to a fairly advanced stage in teaching paraphrase and comprehension, together with the meaning of illustration and generalization.

As a result of their metaphorical application, many proverbs widely different in wording have very similar meanings, and this too is a fruitful source of educational material, as may be seen by pairing the following:

Once bitten, twice shy, 526
A burnt child dreads the fire, 65

A stitch in time saves nine, 619
Who repairs not his gutters repairs his whole house, 763
Barking dogs seldom bite, 32
Empty vessels make the most sound, 163
   Enough is as good as a feast, 167
   Moderation in all things, 465
Little strokes fell great oaks, 419
Many a little makes a mickle, 446

Circumstances alter cases, and thus many proverbs appear to contradict each other. A more advanced exercise consists of pairing contradictory ones and trying to explain how in different circumstances both may be sound. Pairs of this sort include the following:

He who hesitates is lost, 291
Look before you leap, 426
   Too many cooks spoil the broth, 695
   Many hands make light work, 447
Fine feathers make fine birds, 206
Clothes do not make the man, 86
   Absence makes the heart grow fonder, 1
   Out of sight, out of mind, 550
Faint heart ne'er won fair lady, 201
Hew not too high lest the chips fall in thine eye, 303

Their importance

It is easy enough to criticize proverbs. Some for instance seem too cynical. What could be more cynical than *Marriage is a lottery* (450) or *Many kiss the hand they wish to cut off* (448)? Some, like *Every cloud has a silver lining* (171), are too facilely consolatory. Others, like *Call no man happy till he is dead* (68), might be regarded as too crudely defeatist. But proverbs can only be judged as a whole, and as a whole they cover an astonishingly wide range of human experience. The crudest and most repellent in sentiment have in any case disappeared. While times were hard for the common man, his philosophy was inevitably self-consolatory, cynical or defeatist. Proverbs of those times reflected this only too clearly. *Gnaw the bone which is fallen to thy lot* is a typical example. With improving conditions, it is this type of proverb that is fast disappearing.

We are left with a body of proverbs that cannot be brushed to one side as some intellectuals have suggested. They may appear platitudinous to some; but that is merely a result of familiarity. To a child meeting any proverb in this book for the first time it possesses all the charm of a fresh discovery, and it is years, perhaps a lifetime, before that charm is exhausted. It is the same for anyone, however old, who comes to the English language as a foreigner, though in this case it is often a case of old truths being seen in a different light.

After working on this book we are left with the impression that there is little wisdom in this world not covered in one way or another by the proverbs we have collected. Though it would do violence to the finer points, and we would certainly not wish the idea to be pursued too far, most of the wise thoughts so beautifully elaborated by our modern novelists and philosophers can be reduced to the size of a proverb or a combination of proverbs. For as Norman Douglas has pointedly asked:

'What is all wisdom save a collection of platitudes? Take fifty of our current proverbial sayings – they are so trite, so threadbare, that we can hardly bring our lips to utter them. None the less, they embody the concentrated wisdom of the race, and the man who orders his life according to their teaching cannot go far wrong.'

R.R.
C.W.

Alphabetic List of Proverbs
with Explanations

A

1 Absence makes the heart grow fonder
We feel more affection for our relatives and friends when we are
parted from them. A proverb that says just the opposite is OUT OF
SIGHT, OUT OF MIND (550).

2 Accidents will happen in the best-regulated families
Used by Sir Walter Scott in 1823 and still in common use in
modern times, this proverb has a general application and means
that even the most efficient organization is not infallible. It is used
as a consolation for mistakes made.

3 Actions speak louder than words
It is what we do that really matters, not just what we say. In Longfellow's *The Song of Hiawatha*, Hiawatha answers the mighty and
bragging Megissogwen:

> 'Big words do not smite like war-clubs,
> Boastful breath is not a bow-string,
> Taunts are not as sharp as arrows,
> Deeds are better things than words are,
> Actions mightier than boastings!'

Similar proverbs are DEEDS, NOT WORDS (106); FINE WORDS
BUTTER NO PARSNIPS (207); THE GREATEST TALKERS ARE THE
LEAST DOERS (256); HE WHO GIVES FAIR WORDS FEEDS YOU WITH
AN EMPTY SPOON (288); A LITTLE HELP IS WORTH A DEAL OF
PITY (416); PRAISE WITHOUT PROFIT PUTS LITTLE IN THE POT
(565).

4 Adam's ale is the best brew
This tells us that water is the best drink. It is advice against
drinking alcohol. Adam's ale is the old term for water.

5 Advice when most needed is least heeded
Advice is something that wise men don't need and foolish people
won't take; and the greater the need for advice, the less likely the
foolish person is to heed it – that is, to pay careful attention to it.

6 After a storm comes a calm
This optimistically suggests that, just as there is inevitably a calm
after every storm, there must be something better after every piece
of unpleasantness.

7 All are not thieves that dogs bark at
Beware of judging people by appearances. An honest man may
give the impression that he is the biggest scoundrel in the world.
Good looks do not always go with virtue, or ugliness with sin.
  See also NEVER JUDGE BY APPEARANCES (487).

8 All cats are grey in the dark
This suggests that beauty is unimportant. Beneath the outward
appearance people are all much alike. 'When the candles are out,'
wrote Plutarch, 'all women are fair.'

9 All good things come to an end
Pleasures cannot go on for ever, for all things change, and THE
BEST OF FRIENDS MUST PART (41).

10 All's fair in love and war
This proverb would have us believe that in courtship, just as on
the battlefield, it is permissible to use every stratagem and take
advantage of every opportunity. When, for example, a suitor
causes his rival to look foolish in the eyes of the girl they are both
in love with, he can justify his conduct by saying: 'All's fair in
love and war.'

11 All's fish that comes to the net
A professional fisherman can find some use for all the fish he
pulls out of the sea; he cannot afford to be too particular. The
proverb advises us to follow his example by taking advantage of
everything that comes our way. If a dealer in second-hand furniture seems to make a profit out of everything he buys and resells,
however useless it may appear to us, we can say of him: 'All's fish
that comes to his net.'

A similar proverb is ALL'S GRIST THAT COMES TO THE MILL. Grist is corn brought to the mill for grinding. Without grist the mill lies idle and yields no profit for the miller. Figuratively 'to bring grist to the mill' is to bring business or advantage, whilst 'All's grist that comes to the mill' means that use will be made of everything received.

'Do you think,' a wife asked her husband, 'that Mr McKenzie could do with this old suit of yours?'

'Old Mac will take anything! All's grist that comes to *his* mill!'

12   All's well that ends well

It is the end that matters, making up for previous failures and disappointments. Shakespeare used the proverb for the title of one of his comedies.

13   All lay loads on a willing horse

In the days when horses were much used for carrying burdens on their backs, the animals that gave the least trouble were given more work to do than those which were stubborn or intractable. Today a 'willing horse' is a person who is so good-natured and helpful that everyone takes advantage of him.

'I daren't ask old Morgan to do this for us. He always says he can't spare the time – and gets quite nasty when you try to persuade him.'

'Young Simpson's a willing horse. Try him. He's got less time to spare than most, but he doesn't make such a fuss.'

14   All roads lead to Rome

Towards the end of the fourteenth century Chaucer wrote in a treatise on the astrolabe, an ancient astronomical instrument, that 'diverse paths lead diverse folk the right way to Rome'. From this and other references to the many roads to Rome has developed the proverb meaning that a number of persons – scientists, perhaps – can arrive at one common objective by different means.

15   All that glitters is not gold

Do not judge a thing by its attractive appearance. As another proverb (19) reminds us, APPEARANCES ARE DECEPTIVE.

'Why did you believe him when he said he wasn't married?' asked Mary.

'Because,' replied Pamela, 'he was so good-looking and well-dressed, and had such a nice voice.'

'All that glitters is not gold,' Mary reminded her.

16   All things are difficult before they are easy
When first we try to ride a bicycle we are quite sure that we shall never do anything but fall off; but as we go on practising, the whole thing becomes so easy that we wonder why we ever had any difficulty at all.

Similar proverbs are IF AT FIRST YOU DON'T SUCCEED, TRY, TRY, TRY AGAIN (320); LEARN TO WALK BEFORE YOU RUN (389); PRACTICE MAKES PERFECT (562).

17   All work and no play makes Jack a dull boy
We should not always be working. Unless we can enjoy some form of recreation, we become stale and our work suffers in consequence.

'I really think Andrew shouldn't waste his time playing tennis when he ought to be studying for his examinations.'

'But he must have some sort of break. Then he goes back to his books mentally refreshed. This isn't a case of all play and no work, don't forget!'

A somewhat simiar proverb is VARIETY IS THE SPICE OF LIFE (708).

18   Any port in a storm
In times of difficulty or danger any refuge is better than none.

'What a dirty, dingy, miserable old pub to stay the night in!' protested Mrs Fussington. 'No hot water and the paper peeling off the bedroom walls. Can't we do better than this?'

'I'm sorry, dear,' replied her husband, 'but all the other places are full and we may have to drive for miles before we find anywhere else. Let's stop where we are. Any port in a storm.'

A somewhat similar proverb is HALF A LOAF IS BETTER THAN NO BREAD (258).

19   Appearances are deceptive
This means the same as ALL THAT GLITTERS IS NOT GOLD (15). See also NEVER JUDGE BY APPEARANCES (487).

20 The apples on the other side of the wall are the sweetest
Our neighbour's apples may be no larger and riper than our own,
but they always appear to be so. Even on our own tree the best
apples seem to be high up and out of our reach. And this doesn't
apply only to apples, so the proverb means that anything we can't
get seems to be better than what we have.

'That's a fine trout you've caught, uncle,' said Brian admiringly.

'Not too bad, my boy, but you should have seen the one that
got away!'

Betty Collins had the same weakness.

'Why,' she asked her mother, 'do you always give Susan a
bigger slice of cake than you do me?'

'I like that!' protested her sister. 'Mine's much smaller than
yours.'

'Then change plates,' suggested Mrs Collins, adding when they
had done this: 'Now you're both satisfied.'

But they weren't: each thought she had got the worst of the
exchange.

See also FORBIDDEN FRUIT IS SWEETEST (220).

21 Art is long, life is short
This proverb is frequently misunderstood. It does not mean:
'Human life is short, but art goes on for ever.' Its real meaning is:
'There is so much art to learn and so little time to learn it in.' Art
is not used in the popular sense of painting, sculpture, etc. In the
original saying of Hippocrates, the Greek surgeon, it referred to
the art of healing: 'Life is short, the art long, opportunity fleeting
. . .' Art is skill, craft. Chaucer wrote: 'The life is short, the craft
so long to learn.' Sir John Davies wrote:

> Skill comes so slow, as life so fast doth fly,
> We learn so little and forget so much.

22 As well be hanged for a sheep as a lamb
In olden times a person found guilty of sheep-stealing was sen-
tenced to death. Because stealing a lamb was as great a crime as
stealing a sheep and the penalty was the same, the thief might just
as well steal the larger animal and so have more meat for himself
and his family. The modern meaing of the proverb is similar to IN
FOR A PENNY, IN FOR A POUND (342).

'Dad said I was to be home from the dance by eleven o'clock,

but I enjoyed myself so much that it was midnight before I realized
it, so I thought I might as well be hanged for a sheep as a lamb
and stopped on till the end.'

23 As you make your bed, so you must lie in it
Should you make your bed badly, you will probably have an uncomfortable night, for which you will have only yourself to blame.
In much the same way, all of us are responsible for the consequences of our actions, so we must put up with them.

24 As you sow, so shall you reap
You will be punished or rewarded according to whether you have
led a virtuous or a sinful life. The source of the proverb is Galatians,
v, 7: 'Whatsoever a man soweth, that shall he also reap.'

   This is the religious meaning, but it has a wider application in
which it means the same as AS YOU MAKE YOUR BED, SO YOU MUST
LIE IN IT (23).

25 Ask no questions and be told no lies
This is often the reply of parents to children who ask too many
awkward questions.

26 Avoid a questioner, for he is also a tattler
A person who asks a lot of questions will waste no time in passing
your answers on to other people, however confidential they may
be.

B

27 Bad news travels fast
The old proverb was ILL NEWS COMES APACE (337). By this we
mean that bad news nearly always reaches us more quickly than
good news. See also NO NEWS IS GOOD NEWS (508).

28 A bad penny always comes back
If we try to get rid of a counterfeit coin by passing it off upon
somebody else, sooner or later it will find its way back into our
pocket. Figuratively a bad penny is a ne'er-do-well, the black
sheep of the family (649). We use the proverb in reference to a

young man who leaves home in disgrace and returns there after a long absence in the hope that all is forgiven.

A man said to his companion in a public house:

'Who's that down-at-heel fellow propped against the bar? I seem to know his face.'

'Don't you remember him? That's Alec Palmer, the drunken oaf. His father threw him out years ago. When the old man died he sneaked back home to live rent-free and spend his mother's pension on beer. A bad penny if ever there was one.'

29 A bad shearer never had a good sickle
This means the same as A BAD WORKMAN ALWAYS BLAMES HIS TOOLS (30).

30 A bad workman always blames his tools
Good workmanship depends no more on the quality of the tools than it does on the way in which they are used, so to blame the tools for bad workmanship is to attempt to excuse one's own lack of skill. For example: 'I lost the match because my racket needed re-stringing.' 'My essay wasn't very good because I had to use someone else's pen.' 'How did you expect me to catch fish with this rod?' To all these the response could be: 'A bad workman always blames his tools.'

31 The bait hides the hook
It is the hook that catches the fish, but it is the bait that tempts it to take the hook into its mouth. The moral is: beware of an attractive offer, for there is very likely to be a catch in it.

32 Barking dogs seldom bite
When a dog barks at you, this does not necessarily mean that he intends to bite you. He may be just excited or frightened of you. The proverb means that a man who utters threats in a loud voice, or is given to noisy boasting, need not be taken seriously.

33 Be just before you are generous
You have no right to be generous till you have first met the demands of justness. You should not, for example, start giving presents to your friends before you have paid back the money you owe others.

34   The beaten road is the safest

Don't take unnecessary risks. Profit from the experience of others.
The proverb can be better understood if for 'beaten road' we read
'beaten track' or 'well-worn path'. It is safer to keep to such a
path leading through the woods, however much it winds, than to
leave it and try to find a more direct route. The path is well worn
and many people must have passed that way, so it is safe for us
to do the same.

A similar proverb is THE LONGEST WAY ROUND IS THE NEAREST
WAY HOME (425).

35   Beauty is but skin deep

We cannot judge by looks alone. Physical beauty may hide an
ugly nature.

36   Beauty is in the eye of the beholder

'Beauty,' the dictionary tells us, 'is a combination of qualities, as
shape, proportion, colour, in human face or form, or in other
objects, that delights the sight.' The last four words are important.
Beauty does not exist by itself; it exists only in the consciousness
of those who see it. If anything delights the sight of one person,
then it is beautiful to him; if the same thing does not delight the
sight of another person, then it is not beautiful to him.

Similar proverbs are EVERYONE TO HIS TASTE (188); ONE MAN'S
MEAT IS ANOTHER MAN'S POISON (535); TASTES DIFFER (642);
THERE IS NO DISPUTING ABOUT TASTES (657).

37   Beggars must not be choosers

A person who is hungry and has no money to buy food should
not complain when he is offered bread and cheese instead of roast
lamb and new potatoes, with apple tart and cream to follow. He
is in no position to argue with his benefactor and should be grate-
ful for anything he is given. The proverb, of course, goes beyond
food and begging. It refers to anybody whose circumstances are
such that he has no choice in a matter. He must take it or leave it.
Similar proverbs are NEVER LOOK A GIFT HORSE IN THE MOUTH
(488); HE WHO PAYS THE PIPER CALLS THE TUNE (293).

38   The best fish swim near the bottom

They are therefore the most difficult to catch. Nothing is really worth having if it can be got without any trouble. The best things are hard to come by.

39   Best is cheapest
Articles of the best quality usually last longer and give better service than those that are cheap and inferior, so that in the long run they prove cheaper. It does not, however, necessarily follow that the dearest is the best, since some dear things are over-priced.

40   The best is often the enemy of the good
This suggests that in striving to reach perfection we often spoil what would have been good enough. It is thus opposite in advice to IF A THING IS WORTH DOING IT IS WORTH DOING WELL (319).

41   The best of friends must part
This is on the same theme as ALL GOOD THINGS COME TO AN END (9). The words can be found in the chorus of *There is a Tavern in the Town*:

> Fare thee well, for I must leave thee,
> Do not let this parting grieve thee,
> And remember that the best of friends must part.
> Adieu, kind friends, adieu, adieu, adieu, adieu,
> I can no longer stay with you;
> I'll hang my harp on a weeping willow tree,
> And may the world go well with thee.

In passing, to hang one's harp on a willow tree is to put an end to song and mirth. The source is Psalms, cxxxvii, 2.

42   Better an egg today than a hen tomorrow
This means the same as A BIRD IN THE HAND IS WORTH TWO IN THE BUSH (52).

43   Better be a fool than a knave
Of the two evils foolishness is the lesser, since it is usually considered something you are born with, whilst knavery is something a person does deliberately. Moreover, knavery is more likely to land you in prison than is foolishness.

44   Better be an old man's darling than a young man's slave
This proverb suggests, rightly or wrongly, that the woman who

marries an old man will fare better than the woman who marries a young one, on the grounds that the old man is likely to make a great fuss of his young wife, while the young man will expect her to make a fuss of him.

45 Better be sure than sorry

Here 'sure' is used in the old sense of 'safe, free from danger'. 'If we reach the forest,' says a character in Shakespeare, 'we shall be sure enough.' So the literal meaning of the proverb is: 'It is better to be safe than to do anything that may place us in a dangerous position.'

Two boys were chased across a field by a bull. They just managed to escape its horns by climbing up a tree. After half an hour or so one said:

'We can't stop here all day. Let's make a run for it.'

'You do as you like,' said the other. 'I'm stopping where I am till the farmer comes. Better be sure than sorry.'

46 Better be the head of a dog than the tail of a lion

Another old proverb says the same thing more clearly: 'Better be the head of the yeomanry than the tail of the gentry.' In other words, it's better to hold a high position at a low level than to hold a low position at a high level.

'They've thrown me out of the first team,' said Fred, 'and made me captain of the second.'

'You should be glad about that,' smiled his friend. 'Better be the head of a dog than the tail of a lion.'

47 Better bend than break

The pliant tree bends before the wind and is not damaged by the storm, but the rigid tree is often snapped. In the same way it is sometimes better to give way to the wishes of those in authority than to stand up to them and be ruined. This is cowardly advice, unless it is assumed that by such action one lives to fight another day.

Similar proverbs are DISCRETION IS THE BETTER PART OF VALOUR (117); HE THAT FIGHTS AND RUNS AWAY MAY LIVE TO FIGHT ANOTHER DAY (273); ONE PAIR OF HEELS IS OFTEN WORTH TWO PAIRS OF HANDS (539).

48   Better late than never

It is better to do a thing after much procrastination than not to do it at all. It is often used as a semi-humorous excuse, e.g. 'Dear Tom, – I'm sorry I've not written for such a long time, but better late than never . . .' A longer version of the original Latin proverb is: 'Better late than never, but better never late.' See PUNCTUALITY IS THE POLITENESS OF KINGS (574).

49   Better the devil you know than the devil you don't know

An unknown danger or hardship is much more frightening than one we have already experienced.

'I've got to go to Paris again on business next week. The very thought of crossing the Channel makes me feel seasick.'

'Why don't you go by air?'

'I daren't. I'd be scared to death.'

50   Better to ask the way than go astray

Some people are too proud to admit that they don't know, and, by refusing to ask, go astray. That is to say, they do the wrong thing or become lost. The proverb advises us to pocket our pride and ask for advice in order to avoid such unnecessary consequences.

51   Between two stools you fall to the ground

If you cannot make up your mind which of two things to do, you are liable to get yourself into difficulties by doing neither. If a car comes suddenly round the corner and you cannot decide which way to jump, the car will hit you, particularly if the driver is suffering from a similar indecision!

Dr Brewer explained that the allusion is to a practical joke (called 'Ambassador') played on greenhorns at sea. 'A tub full of water is placed between two stools, and the whole being covered with a green cloth, a sailor sits on each stool, to keep the cloth tight. The two sailors represent Neptune and Amphitrite, and the greenhorn, as ambassador, is introduced to their majesties. He is given the seat of honour between them; but no sooner does he take his seat than the two sailors rise, and the greenhorn falls into the tub, amidst the laughter of the whole crew.'

A similar proverb is IF YOU RUN AFTER TWO HARES YOU WILL CATCH NEITHER (333).

52 A bird in the hand is worth two in the bush
If a hunter has shot one bird, he should be satisfied with that and
not go off looking for the ones that flew away.

We use the proverb to mean that it is better to accept something small than to reject it and hope to get more later on.

'The antique dealer said I *might* get ten pounds for the vase if I
took it up to London, but he himself wasn't prepared to give me
more than a fiver for it. A bird in the hand, I thought, and accepted his offer.'

53 Birds in their little nests agree
This comes from *Love Between Brothers and Sisters*, one of the
Divine Songs for Children by Isaac Watts. The practical application of the proverb is that if they don't agree some hapless
nestling is going to be pushed out and killed. The same applies in
a figurative sense to human families and communities; if they
wish to be happy they must live together in harmony.

54 Birds of a feather flock together
Here 'of a feather' means 'of the same kind or family', and the
verb 'to flock' means 'to feed or travel in company'. We do not
find rooks flocking with swallows, or partridges flocking with
seagulls. In the same way, human beings with similar tastes or
interests tend to come together in groups. The proverb is often
used about people we disapprove of.

'They're a rough crowd. Why does young Robinson have anything to do with them?'

'Birds of a feather flock together, you know.'

Similar proverbs are LIKE WILL TO LIKE (411); MEN ARE
KNOWN BY THE COMPANY THEY KEEP (455). Proverbs dealing
with the dangers of keeping bad company are HE SHOULD HAVE
A LONG SPOON THAT SUPS WITH THE DEVIL (270); HE THAT
TOUCHETH PITCH SHALL BE DEFILED (279); THE ROTTEN APPLE
INJURES ITS NEIGHBOURS (590); WHO KEEPS COMPANY WITH
THE WOLF WILL LEARN TO HOWL (762).

55 The biter is sometimes bit
'Biter' is a slang word for a cheat or swindler, e.g. a card-sharper.
When he himself is cheated by his prospective victim, 'the biter is
bit'. In a general way, this refers to any form of retribution. As

Laertes says in Shakespeare's *Hamlet* after being wounded by the rapier that he himself has poisoned, 'I am justly kill'd with my own treachery.'

56 Blessed is he who expects nothing, for he shall never be disappointed
Don't be too optimistic about the future. Remember that THERE'S MANY A SLIP 'TWIXT THE CUP AND THE LIP (655).

Alexander Pope, who wrote this on 6th October, 1727, in a letter to John Gay, described it as 'a ninth beatitude added to the eighth in the Scripture'. The reference is to Matthew, v, 3–10.

57 Blood is thicker than water
Unlike blood, water soon evaporates when it is spilt, and leaves no trace afterwards. Figuratively 'blood' means 'relationship'. When we say that persons are of the same blood, we mean that they are descended from the same ancestors. The interest we take in those not so close to us as blood relations can be compared to water, which is thinner and less enduring. So says the proverb, though the reality is not always in accord with it! 'God gave us relatives,' said the cynic. 'Thank God, we can choose our friends.' Kinship, however, is a very strong tie, and help is often given not for the sake of the individual but for the sake of the family.

'I've never had much patience with that nephew of mine, but his mother is my sister, so I paid the fine to keep the young fool out of prison.'

58 Books and friends should be few but good
People who have too many books often find they haven't any time to read them. In the same way, people with too many friends cannot find enough time to cultivate friendship with all of them. It is therefore better that both friends and books should be few in number and good in quality.

59 Boys will be boys
'Boys are boys,' said the Latin proverb, 'and employ themselves with boyish matters.' These matters are normally noisy, destructive and dangerous, and when we encounter any of these signs of healthy boyhood – a broken window, perhaps, or a cat with its head pushed into a salmon tin – we shrug our shoulders and murmur, 'Boys will be boys.'

60 Bread is the staff of life

Here 'bread' refers to food in general, as in the Lord's Prayer ('Give us this day our daily bread'); and 'staff' is something that serves as a stay or support. Hence food supports life, and man cannot live without it.

See also AN EMPTY SACK CANNOT STAND UPRIGHT (162).

61 Brevity is the soul of wit

This was already a proverb in Shakespeare's time. In his *Hamlet* we find the first record of it in literature. Old Polonius is giving King Claudius and Queen Gertrude his opinion of the mental condition of the Queen's son, Hamlet. After saying that time should not be wasted on long preliminaries, he goes on:

> Therefore, since brevity is the soul of wit
> And tediousness the limb and outward flourishes,
> I will be brief. Your noble son is mad ...

It will be seen that 'wit' in this context does not mean 'humour' but 'intelligence, understanding' in the sense of knowing how to pass on information. When we use the expression we mean 'wit' in its other sense, which is the power to express oneself in a clever, humorous way.

A witty remark or retort is all the better for being short. Here is an example:

'How would you like your hair cut, sir?' asked the talkative hairdresser.

'If possible in silence,' replied the customer.

62 The bull must be taken by the horns

In moments of danger during a bullfight, a strong, expert matador will grasp the bull by the horns and so prevent it from tossing him.

By extension the proverb means that when faced by perils or difficulties we should meet them fearlessly, not try to evade them.

As the jeep rounded the bend, the soldiers in it saw that the road ahead was blocked by a mob of rebels.

'What do I do now?' asked the driver.

'Step on it,' said the corporal in charge, 'and cut straight through 'em.'

The driver brought down his foot on the accelerator, the jeep shot forward, the insurgents broke up in disorder and scrambled up the banks on either side of the road.

'Always take the bull by the horns,' said the corporal with a satisfied grin as they continued on their way.

A similar proverb is HE WHO HANDLES A NETTLE TENDERLY IS SOONEST STUNG (290).

63   A bully is always a coward
A bully finds his victims among those who are weaker and smaller than he is, because he hasn't the courage to attack anyone his own size.

64   Burn not your house to fright the mouse away
Don't take extreme measures to get rid of something quite trivial. A similar proverb is TAKE NOT A MUSKET TO KILL A BUTTERFLY (633).

65   A burnt child dreads the fire
Once he has burnt himself he is very careful to see that it doesn't happen again. Any such painful experience is not soon forgotten. A similar proverb is ONCE BITTEN, TWICE SHY (526).

66   Busiest men find the most time
People who do a lot are the people who have most energy. However busy they are, they can usually manage to do something more. It follows from this that IDLE FOLK HAVE THE LEAST LEISURE (317).

C

67   Call a spade a spade
Speak plainly and to the point, saying exactly what you mean and using the simplest terms. In Arnold Bennett's novel, *The Card*, published in 1911, Mrs Machin says:

'Ye can call it influenza if ye like. There was no influenza in my young days. We called a cold a cold.'

68   Call no man happy till he is dead
This cynical proverb suggests that life is bound to be so bad that no living person can ever be happy.

69 Care killed a cat

Care is a load on the mind. If it killed a cat, which has nine lives –
or so 'tis said – it will kill *you*, who have only one life. So don't
worry – get that load off your mind. George Wither, the Jacobean
poet, wrote of Christmas:

> Hang sorrow! Care will kill a cat,
> And therefore let's be merry.

70 Cast ne'er a clout till May is out

Early spring in Britain often turns warm for a few days. But if you
start leaving off clothes you will run a risk, as it may become very
cold again – right up to the end of May. 'Cast a clout' is an old
way of saying 'leave off clothes'.

71 Cast not the first stone

Before condemning anyone who has done wrong, ask yourself
whether your own conduct has been blameless.

The proverb derives from the story told in Chapter VIII of the
Gospel according to St John.

While Jesus was teaching in the temple the scribes and Pharisees
brought before Him a woman taken in adultery.

'Moses in the law commanded that such should be stoned: but
what sayest thou?' they asked.

Jesus replied: 'He that is without sin among you, let him first
cast a stone at her.'

Those who heard this, 'being convicted by their own conscience',
went out one by one until Jesus was left alone with the woman.

He asked her: 'Woman, where are those thine accusers? hath
no man condemned thee?'

'No man, Lord.'

'Neither do I condemn thee: go, and sin no more.'

72 A cat has nine lives

This is another way of saying that a cat is much more likely to
escape death than are most animals. It is too wily and agile to be
taken by surprise, and even when it falls it manages to come down
on its feet, which are sufficiently padded to break the shock.

The proverb is used rather loosely in such contexts as:

'She's had so many accidents with her new car that I wonder
she's not been killed.'

'A cat has nine lives.'

Whether there is any play on the word 'cat' in the sense of 'spiteful woman' depends on the feelings of the speaker!

73   A cat may look at a king

> A cat may look at a King
> And surely I may look at an ugly thing.

This is one of Mother Goose's Nursery Rhymes. It means: 'If a cat may look at a king, I have as much right to take an interest in what *you* are doing. Are you so important that I can't even look at you?'

74   Catch as catch can

Get all you can by whatever means you have at your disposal. A youth who makes a living by begging and running errands can be said to lead a catch-as-catch-can existence.

The phrase comes from the style of wrestling in which all holds are permitted except those that may be barred by mutual consent.

75   Catch not at the shadow and lose the substance

This warns us against wasting time on trivial aspects of a matter, because in doing so we may neglect the essential matter itself.

76   Catch your bear before you sell its skin

This is another way of saying NEVER SPEND YOUR MONEY BEFORE YOU HAVE IT (493). Act prudently and don't be over-optimistic. Similar proverbs are DON'T COUNT YOUR CHICKENS BEFORE THEY ARE HATCHED (124); DO NOT HALLOO TILL YOU ARE OUT OF THE WOOD (131); FIRST CATCH YOUR HARE (210); THERE'S MANY A SLIP 'TWIXT THE CUP AND THE LIP (655).

77   Caveat emptor

This is one of those proverbs that have remained more common in their original form than in the English translation. It is the Latin for LET THE BUYER BEWARE (398).

78   Charity begins at home

This proverb is often used as an excuse for not helping those outside the family circle.

'I found myself being asked for subscriptions to so many good causes that it was costing me more than I could really afford, so now I give nothing to any of them. After all, charity begins at home.'

But that is not the real meaning of the proverb. In its literal sense charity is Christian love of one's fellow men; kindness; natural affection. If children learn to love and help those nearest to them in their early years, they will love and help their fellow men when they grow up. In other words, charity begins at home, but it does not end there.

79 Charity covers a multitude of sins

By this we mean that some who give money away do so only to soothe their own uneasy consciences. But here again this is not the true meaning, for charity is Christian love.

The original wording is to be found in I Peter, iv, 8: 'And above all things have fervent charity among yourselves: for charity shall cover the multitude of sins.' James Moffatt renders this: 'Above all, be keen to love one another, for love hides a host of sins.'

80 Cherchez la femme

This is one of those proverbs that have remained more common in their original form than in the English translation. It is the French for 'Find the woman' and means that whenever there is any trouble there is usually a woman behind it.

81 The child is father of the man

This inversion of the natural order of things means that by studying the character of a child we can tell what sort of a man he is going to be. As Milton wrote in *Paradise Regained*: 'The childhood shows the man, as morning shows the day.'

The source of the proverb is a short poem by Wordsworth.

> My heart leaps up when I behold
>   A rainbow in the sky:
> So was it when my life began,
> So is it now I am a man,
> So be it when I shall grow old
>   Or let me die!
> The Child is father of the Man:
> And I could wish my days to be
> Bound each to each by natural piety.

82 Children should be seen and not heard

Children should be silent in the presence of their elders and not speak until they are spoken to. If only the kids would understand this!

See also WHEN CHILDREN STAND QUIET THEY HAVE DONE SOME ILL (743).

83 Christmas comes but once a year

Because the Christmas festival comes only once a year, it is suggested that we ought to be tolerant and overlook people's riotous behaviour – too much eating, drinking, spending. Equally, because it is only once a year that we are given the opportunity, we ought also to do good – give presents, help the poor, and so on.

84 Circumstances alter cases

Here 'case' has the meaning of situation, the position in which one finds oneself; and this position is determined by the circumstances surrounding it. If the circumstances change, the situation (i.e. the case) changes also.

We can, for instance, take the case of Mr Gregson, a well-to-do bachelor with a large house, who agreed with his friend Mr Eddy that this second gentleman should occupy the whole of the top floor rent free. Then Mr Gregson lost most of his fortune in a disastrous business venture and was forced to tell Mr Eddy that he had no alternative but to charge him three pounds a week for the rooms he occupied. When Mr Eddy reminded him of their original agreement, Mr Gregson claimed that circumstances alter cases – that the situation had changed.

See also WATER IS A BOON IN THE DESERT, BUT THE DROWNING MAN CURSES IT (717).

85 Cleanliness is next to godliness

Cleanliness can be defined as 'diligence in keeping clean in person and dress'; and 'next to' means 'second only to'. Francis Bacon wrote in his *Advancement of Learning*: 'Cleanliness of the body was ever deemed to proceed from a due reverence to God.' The axiom certainly dates back to very ancient times.

86 Clothes do not make the man

It is what is behind the man – that is, his character – that really matters. On the other hand, this is contradicted by THE TAILOR

MAKES THE MAN (630) and FINE FEATHERS MAKE FINE BIRDS (206).

87 Coming events cast their shadows before

As Cicero wrote: 'Certain signs precede certain events.' For example, the widening by the Germans of the Kiel Canal in 1909 to admit the passage of modern battleships was a sign preceding the outbreak of World War I in 1914.

The proverb is a quotation from Thomas Campbell's *Lochiel's Warning*. The Wizard is telling Sir Donald Cameron of Lochiel in advance of the victory of the English over the Scots, led by Bonnie Prince Charlie, the Young Pretender, at Culloden Moor in 1746.

> Lochiel, Lochiel! beware of the day;
> For, dark and despairing, my sight I may seal,
> But man cannot cover what God will reveal.
> 'Tis the sunset of life gives me mystical lore,
> And coming events cast their shadows before.
> I tell thee Culloden's dread echoes shall ring
> For the bloodhounds that bark for thy fugitive king.

See also A STRAW WILL SHOW WHICH WAY THE WIND BLOWS (621).

88 Comparisons are odious

This proverb dates back to the fifteenth century. It means that we should not make comparisons between two people, because it is very likely unjust to one or other of them – or to both. To say that Mr Smith is a better man than Mr Brown because he goes to church on Sundays is to suggest that Mr Brown is wicked, which may be completely untrue.

89 Conscience does make cowards of us all

This is a quotation from Hamlet's famous soliloquy beginning 'To be or not to be . . .' We use it as a proverb to mean that anyone who has a guilty conscience is frightened of everything.

A similar proverb is HE THAT COMMITS A FAULT THINKS EVERYONE SPEAKS OF IT (272).

90 Constant dripping wears away the stone

Sometimes 'dropping' is used instead of 'dripping'. The lesson to be learnt is summed up in the last two words of this quotation from Ovid: 'What is harder than rock, or softer than water? Yet soft water hollows out hard rock. Only persevere.'

Other proverbs on this theme are IF AT FIRST YOU DON'T SUCCEED, TRY, TRY, TRY AGAIN (320); IT'S DOGGED THAT DOES IT (356); LITTLE BY LITTLE AND BIT BY BIT (415); LITTLE STROKES FELL GREAT OAKS (419); ROME WAS NOT BUILT IN A DAY (588); SLOW BUT SURE WINS THE RACE (603); WHERE THERE'S A WILL THERE'S A WAY (755).

91 A constant guest is never welcome
People like their friends' company at fairly long intervals. If their friends come too often they are apt to grow to dislike them. See also DO NOT WEAR OUT YOUR WELCOME (150).

92 A contented mind is a perpetual feast
This means that contentment of mind is the cause of lasting happiness, and suggests that striving for such contentment is more important than striving for material riches.

93 The course of true love never did run smooth
When two young people love each other dearly they often have difficulties to face before they can marry. The proverb is a quotation from Shakespeare's *A Midsummer Night's Dream*. The words are spoken by Lysander, who is in love with Hermia, whose father has commanded her to marry Demetrius, a young man of noble family. All ends happily.

94 Courtesy costs nothing
There is nothing to be lost by behaving in a courteous way. Sometimes 'civility' or 'politeness' is used instead of 'courtesy'. Another version is THERE IS NOTHING THAT COSTS LESS THAN CIVILITY (670).

95 Cowards die many times before their deaths
This proverb is a quotation from Shakespeare's *Julius Caesar*. Caesar says:

> Cowards die many times before their deaths;
> The valiant never tastes of death but once.

A coward often imagines that he is on the point of death when he is not, with the result that, unlike a brave man, he frequently experiences the fear of dying.

96 The cowl does not make the monk
A cowl is a long cloak with a hood that covers the head of the wearer. The proverb means that the wearing of such a garment does not turn a man into a monk; he may be a rascal disguised as a holy man – a 'wolf in sheep's clothing'. The moral is contained in another proverb, NEVER JUDGE BY APPEARANCES (487).

97 A creaking gate hangs long
Persons in weak health often live a long time.

98 Cross the stream where it is shallowest
Don't make difficulties for yourself by doing things the hard way. Find the simplest means of achieving your object.

99 Curses, like chickens, come home to roost
Here 'come home to roost' means 'recoil upon the originator', just as when a stone thrown up into the air comes down on the head of the thrower. A curse is the utterance of an evil wish, e.g. 'May you be run over by a bus!' The proverb means that curses are less likely to injure the person cursed than the curser himself – it is he who is run over by a bus.

100 Custom makes all things easy
This means the same as PRACTICE MAKES PERFECT (562).

101 Custom reconciles us to everything
In modern parlance, we can get used to anything. The longer we have to put up with it, however irksome or unpleasant it may be, the more able are we to adapt ourselves to it. It becomes part of our life and we accept it as such. For example, if we move into a house near a factory that keeps going twenty-four hours a day, at first the noise of the machinery keeps us awake at night, but as time goes by we get used to it, perhaps unable to sleep without it.

102 Cut your coat according to your cloth
Adjust your expenditure according to your resources.
  'I asked the dealer the price of the tennis racket I had set my heart on, but it was too expensive, so I had to cut my coat according to my cloth and buy a cheaper one.'
  See also STRETCH YOUR LEGS ACCORDING TO YOUR COVERLET (623).

D

103   The darkest hour is that before the dawn
Even when things seem at their very worst, they may shortly
improve.

A similar proverb is IT'S A LONG LANE THAT HAS NO TURNING
(349).

104   Dead men tell no tales
Death silences a man for ever. If he knows something in his lifetime that others do not want made public, he cannot reveal their
secret when he is dead, so they are safe. In a seventeenth-century
play called *Andronicus Commenius* by John Wilson one of the
characters says: "Twere best to knock them in the head . . . The
dead do tell no tales.'

105   Death is the great leveller
There can be no such distinctions as wealth, poverty, greatness,
humbleness among the dead. When dead we lose all our worldly
attributes. In this sense death makes us all equal.

106   Deeds, not words
A person is known and judged more by his actions than by what
he says. This is another form of ACTIONS SPEAK LOUDER THAN
WORDS (3).

107   Desert and reward seldom keep company
Those deserving of reward do not often receive it. The reward is
not necessarily a payment in cash. The proverb can mean that
those most deserving of recognition are frequently overlooked or
neglected, whilst others receive the praise.

108   Desires are nourished by delays
The longer we are kept waiting for something, the more we want
it.

109   Desperate diseases must have desperate remedies
Some forms of medical treatment are not normally used because
they are liable to be as dangerous in effect as the diseases themselves. But when a patient's condition is so grave that his life is

almost despaired of, there is no alternative but to take a fifty-fifty chance and use one of those desperate remedies.

In the same way, if a man finds himself in a desperate position, he must take desperate steps to get out of it. For example, should a gambler be deeply in debt, he may rob his employers of a thousand pounds, giving as his excuse when charged with the embezzlement, 'I couldn't help myself. Desperate diseases must have desperate remedies.'

110   The devil can cite Scripture for his purpose

This is an attack on hypocrisy, on those who cover up their evil-doing by quoting passages from the Bible. The proverb comes from Shakespeare's *The Merchant of Venice*:

> The devil can cite Scripture for his purpose.
> An evil soul, producing holy witness,
> Is like a villain with a smiling cheek,
> A goodly apple, rotten at the heart:
> O, what a goodly outside falsehood hath!

The following, from *Richard III*, also applies:

> But then I sigh; and, with a piece of Scripture,
> Tell them that God bids us do good for evil:
> And thus I clothe my naked villainy
> With old odd ends, stolen out of holy writ;
> And seem a saint, when most I play the devil.

111   The devil finds work for idle hands to do

Those who have nothing useful to do and seek some way of passing the time are liable to drift into wrongdoing.

112   The devil is not so black as he is painted

No one is wholly bad, and when we think that someone has been blamed too much we use this proverb.

'I agree with you up to a point, but don't be too hard on him. The devil is not so black as he is painted.'

A similar proverb is GIVE THE DEVIL HIS DUE (236).

113   The devil take the hindmost

This is a shortened version of EVERY MAN FOR HIMSELF, AND THE DEVIL TAKE THE HINDMOST (180).

114 The devil was sick . . .

> The devil was sick, the devil a monk would be;
> The devil was well, the devil a monk was he.

People who make pious resolutions in time of illness or peril forget all about them when they are healthy and safe again. John Owen wrote this epigram:

> God and the Doctor we alike adore
> But only when in danger, not before;
> The danger o'er, both are alike requited,
> God is forgotten, and the Doctor slighted.

The phrase 'the devil a monk was he' is a play on words; it does not mean that the devil became a monk, but that he did not. We find it in such other contexts as: 'I asked everybody to attend the meeting, but devil a one turned up.' Nobody came.

115 Diamond cut diamond

This is more usual than 'Diamond cuts diamond'.

Diamond is the hardest substance known; a diamond can be cut only by another diamond. The phrase refers to opponents who are an equal match in wit, cunning or strong-mindedness. Any conclusion reached is not without mutual injury.

See also WHEN GREEK MEETS GREEK, THEN COMES THE TUG OF WAR (744).

116 Discontent is the first step in progress

Were we all completely satisfied with the existing state of affairs, there would be no progress. It is only when we are not content with things as they are that we decide that something must be done to improve them.

117 Discretion is the better part of valour

Although a brave man is better than a coward, caution is often better than rashness.

Tom might say to Harry: 'I dare you to walk along the edge of that cliff.'

Harry might reply: 'Why should I risk my life just to prove that I'm brave? Don't forget that discretion is the better part of valour.'

Similar proverbs are BETTER BEND THAN BREAK (47); HE THAT FIGHTS AND RUNS AWAY MAY LIVE TO FIGHT ANOTHER DAY

(273); ONE PAIR OF HEELS IS OFTEN WORTH TWO PAIRS OF HANDS (539).

118 Distance lends enchantment to the view

This is a quotation from *The Pleasures of Hope* by the Scottish poet, Thomas Campbell:

> 'Tis distance lends enchantment to the view,
> And robes the mountain in its azure hue.

When we get closer to it we may find only ugly rocks, and the mountain no longer enchants us. This is a commentary on life. As another proverb reminds us, EXPECTATION IS BETTER THAN REALIZATION (195). In his poem *Hymen* John Cunningham wrote:

> So various is the human mind;
> Such are the frailties of mankind!
> What at a distance charmed our eyes,
> Upon attainment, droops, and dies.

And if distance lends enchantment, FAMILIARITY BREEDS CONTEMPT (203).

119 Do as I say, not as I do

This is a tilt against those preachers who condemn in the pulpit the very things of which they themselves are guilty. It is also used humorously by those who have been caught out.

'Dad,' said Willie at the breakfast table, 'I thought you told me not to read at meal times. Now you're doing it yourself.'

'Do as I say, Willie, not as I do,' said his father over the top of the newspaper.

See also PRACTISE WHAT YOU PREACH (563).

120 Do as most men do, then most men will speak well of you

Go with the crowd. If you try to act differently from the majority you will become unpopular. Robert Nugent wrote:

> Safer with multitudes to stray,
> Than tread alone a fairer way:
> To mingle with the erring throng,
> Than boldly speak ten millions wrong.

See also THERE IS SAFETY IN NUMBERS (671); WHEN IN ROME DO AS THE ROMANS DO (748).

121 Do as you would be done by
Treat others as you would like them to treat you. If you don't you may be punished, as Tom was in *The Water Babies*, by that fearsome lady, Mrs Bedonebyasyoudid.

This important proverb is regarded by many moralizers, Christian and non-Christian alike, as the essence of good behaviour. The world would be near-perfect if the advice were universally followed.

122 Do not cast your pearls before swine
Do not give a beautiful or precious thing to a person who is totally unable to appreciate its value. The proverb is very often used by those who consider themselves superior beings, more intelligent or gifted than their fellows.

'I read some of my poetry aloud to them, but it was casting pearls before swine. They obviously didn't understand a word of it and soon started yawning, looking at their watches and fidgeting in their chairs.'

The source of the proverb is Matthew, vii, 6:

'Give not that which is holy unto the dogs, neither cast ye your pearls before swine, lest they trample them under their feet, and turn again and rend you.'

123 Don't change horses in mid-stream
Crossing a stream on horseback is not always easy, and to transfer oneself from one horse to another during the process is inviting a ducking, if nothing worse. In the same way, if we think it necessary to make changes, we must choose the right moment to make them.

In 1864, at the height of the American Civil War, there were demands for a change in the presidency. The then president, Abraham Lincoln, replied to his critics:

'I have not permitted myself, gentlemen, to conclude that I am the best man in the country; but I am reminded in this connection of a story of an old Dutch farmer, who remarked to a companion once that it was not best to swap horses when crossing a stream.'

124 Don't count your chickens before they are hatched
It is a mistake to assume that because your hen is sitting on a dozen eggs you will have twelve chickens, since some, perhaps

even all of them, may be bad and not hatch. So never be too optimistic about anything; wait till your difficulties are over before you boast of success.

Mr Smith hoped to be made manager before the end of the year and have his salary greatly increased. He started placing orders for new furniture and a bigger car before the promotion had actually been made.

'Don't count your chickens before they are hatched,' warned his wife.

This was good advice, for it was Mr Jones who was made manager, and Mr Smith found himself in financial difficulties.

Similar proverbs are CATCH YOUR BEAR BEFORE YOU SELL ITS SKIN (76); DO NOT HALLOO TILL YOU ARE OUT OF THE WOOD (131); FIRST CATCH YOUR HARE (210); NEVER SPEND YOUR MONEY BEFORE YOU HAVE IT (493); THERE'S MANY A SLIP 'TWIXT THE CUP AND THE LIP (655).

125 Don't cross a bridge till you come to it

Don't worry about something before it has happened. Your fears may be groundless, for it may never happen.

Similar proverbs are DON'T CRY BEFORE YOU ARE HURT (126); DON'T MEET TROUBLE HALF-WAY (137); NEVER TROUBLE TROUBLE TILL TROUBLE TROUBLES YOU (496); SUFFICIENT UNTO THE DAY IS THE EVIL THEREOF (627).

126 Don't cry before you are hurt

You should not give way to misfortune till it actually happens, since it may not happen. This motherly advice is often given to quarrelling children.

Similar proverbs are DON'T CROSS A BRIDGE TILL YOU COME TO IT (125); DON'T MEET TROUBLE HALF-WAY (137); NEVER TROUBLE TROUBLE TILL TROUBLE TROUBLES YOU (496); SUFFICIENT UNTO THE DAY IS THE EVIL THEREOF (627).

127 Don't cry stinking fish

Here the verb 'to cry' means 'to offer for sale in the street'. Barrow-boys cry fruit: 'Fine ripe strawberries!' Flower-girls cry flowers: 'Lovely violets!' Fishmongers cry fish: 'Fresh-caught mackerel!' But they and others of their kind would not find many customers if they condemned their own wares – 'Overripe strawberries!' and so on.

By extension, to cry stinking fish is to belittle one's own efforts; to speak unfavourably of what one has to offer to others. For example, a young author sent his first novel to a firm of publishers with a covering letter admitting that the grammar was faulty, the construction weak and the plot unoriginal, but he hoped they would accept it for publication. We wonder if they did! Of course, to go to the opposite extreme can be even worse. See SELF-PRAISE IS NO RECOMMENDATION (595).

Other proverbs advising against self-deprecation are DON'T MAKE YOURSELF A MOUSE, OR THE CAT WILL EAT YOU (136); MAKE YOURSELF ALL HONEY AND THE FLIES WILL DEVOUR YOU (439).

128 Don't cut off your nose to spite your face

The verb 'to spite' means 'to be revenged upon'. The advice given here is: 'Don't do anything in a fit of temper that will injure only yourself.'

Mrs White suddenly stopped buying her meat from Mr Rawlings, whose shop was just round the corner from her home, and transferred her custom to a butcher so far away that she had to go by bus.

'Why on earth do that?' asked her neighbour. 'Mr Rawlings's meat is better and cheaper than anyone else's for miles around.'

'I'm doing it,' replied Mrs White, 'because his wife's sister has just been divorced by her husband.'

By going elsewhere and spending her money on bus fares and inferior meat, the intolerant Mrs White caused inconvenience to nobody but herself. No wonder her neighbour accused her of cutting off her nose to spite her face!

129 Don't cut the bough you are standing on

If you depend upon anything, make sure you can do without it before you get rid of it. Don't endanger your own position by a hasty or thoughtless action. Mr Smithers cut off the bough he was standing on by giving his landlord a week's notice before he found somewhere else to live.

130 Don't empty the baby out with the bath water

In achieving your aim (of pouring away the bath water), make sure you don't do something else (pouring away the baby) that more than cancels out your achievement.

A certain Mr Williamson, who had lived for years in London, decided to break with the past and seek a new life overseas. The day before he was due to sail he destroyed a pile of old correspondence, only to discover when it was too late that he had burnt his passport as well. We can say of the careless Mr Williamson that he had emptied the baby out with the bath water.

131   Do not halloo till you are out of the wood

The old verb 'to halloo' meant 'to give a loud exclamation'. Travellers lost in a forest were relieved and delighted when they found their way through it and emerged into the open country; but to mistake a small clearing for the open country and shout 'Hurrah! We're out of the wood!' was rejoicing too soon, for many more trees might lie beyond the clearing.

We use the proverb as a warning against being too optimistic, against celebrating escape from danger before the danger is really over.

'Here comes a helicopter!' cried one of the shipwrecked sailors on the raft. 'We're saved!'

But the light was bad and the pilot did not see them. As the sound of the helicopter died away another sailor said sadly:

'We're not through the wood yet.'

Similar proverbs are CATCH YOUR BEAR BEFORE YOU SELL ITS SKIN (76); DON'T COUNT YOUR CHICKENS BEFORE THEY ARE HATCHED (124); FIRST CATCH YOUR HARE (210); NEVER SPEND YOUR MONEY BEFORE YOU HAVE IT (493); THERE'S MANY A SLIP 'TWIXT THE CUP AND THE LIP (655).

132   Don't have too many irons in the fire

In the days before motor transport, when horses were in great demand, blacksmiths were busy men. The 'irons in the fire' were for forging into horseshoes; and if the blacksmith had a number of horses waiting to be shoed, he might try to save time by putting too many irons in his furnace, so that the heat was insufficient to make them all red-hot.

When we use the proverb we mean that if we attempt to do too much at once, we shall not do anything properly. As another proverb (285) puts it: HE WHO BEGINS MANY THINGS, FINISHES BUT FEW.

133 Do not kick against the pricks
It is futile to fight a losing battle by resisting authority.

A prick is an ox-goad, a spiked stick for urging cattle. Should an animal dislike this treatment and kick out with his hoofs, it will not escape another jab. The saying comes from the ninth chapter of Acts: '. . . it is hard for thee to kick against the pricks.'

We use the proverb in such contexts as this:

'The Town Council have told me to cut down the tree because they think it's dangerous to passers-by. I've refused to do it.'

'You'll be forced to in the end, so why not do it now? It's no use kicking against the pricks.'

Other proverbs on the theme of resignation are WHAT CAN'T BE CURED MUST BE ENDURED (725); WHAT MUST BE MUST BE (736); YOU MUST GRIN AND BEAR IT (794).

134 Don't make a mountain out of a molehill
Don't make a fuss about nothing. Don't turn a trifling matter into a major disaster.

'You've absolutely ruined my new dress by spilling that soup over it.'

'It's only a tiny stain, which can soon be got out. For heaven's sake don't make a mountain out of a molehill!'

See also TAKE NOT A MUSKET TO KILL A BUTTERFLY (633).

135 Don't make a rod for your own back
Don't make a stick with which you yourself may be beaten. In other words, don't do anything that may get you into trouble later on.

'When I offered to start a Youth Club in the town, I didn't know what I was letting myself in for. Talk about making a rod for my own back! It's a whole-time job these days.'

136 Don't make yourself a mouse, or the cat will eat you
If you belittle yourself, people will take advantage of you. Stand up for yourself.

Similar proverbs are DON'T CRY STINKING FISH (127); MAKE YOURSELF ALL HONEY AND THE FLIES WILL DEVOUR YOU (439).

137 Don't meet trouble half-way
Don't worry about something before it has happened. Your fears may be groundless, for it may never happen.

Similar proverbs are DON'T CROSS A BRIDGE TILL YOU COME
TO IT (125); DON'T CRY BEFORE YOU ARE HURT (126); NEVER
TROUBLE TROUBLE TILL TROUBLE TROUBLES YOU (496); SUFFI-
CIENT UNTO THE DAY IS THE EVIL THEREOF (627).

138   Don't outrun the constable
Another version is: 'Don't overrun the constable.' This has
nothing to do with not running faster than a policeman, or
shooting past him when he is on point duty. It means: 'Don't get
into debt.' In olden days police constables acted as debt-collectors.
For example, if a tradesman allowed his customers one month's
credit, and a customer failed to pay at the end of that period, the
tradesman might call in the constable, and the debtor might well
be sent to prison. So 'to outrun the constable' was to go beyond
the point when you were safe from the arm of the law.

139   Don't pour out the dirty water before you have clean
In countries where water is in short supply it has to be carefully
and sparingly used. By extension the proverb means that you
should not discard anything until you have made sure of a re-
placement. For example, don't throw away the stump of a pencil
until you have provided yourself with a new one; if you wish to
jot down an important note while it is fresh in your mind, it is
better to have the stump than no pencil at all.

140   Don't put all your eggs in one basket
'Spread the risk' is the lesson this proverb teaches. Accidents will
happen, so use two baskets and thereby reduce the chance of
losing all your eggs in one go. Similarly, don't keep all your money
in one pocket; distribute it about your person. Then if a pick-
pocket deprives you of your notecase on a crowded train, he does
not rob you of all you have. Again, when investing your capital,
do not venture the whole amount in a single speculation, but
spread it over several. If one fails, you will still have money safely
invested in the others.

A similar proverb is THE MOUSE THAT HAS BUT ONE HOLE IS
QUICKLY TAKEN (474).

141   Do not put new wine into old bottles
At first sight this would seem to imply that it is false economy to
use wine bottles more than once, and that the saying means the

same as, for example, PENNY WISE, POUND FOOLISH. But this is not so. The real meaning is that we should not try to bring together things that are out of keeping with each other. To play dance music at a funeral is to put new wine into old bottles.

Let us consider first the source of the saying, which is Matthew, ix, 17: 'Neither do men put new wine into old bottles: else the bottles break, and the wine runneth out, and the bottles perish: but they put new wine into new bottles, and both are preserved.' These bottles, of course, were not made of glass, but from the skins of goats. Once a wineskin had been stretched by fermenting wine, it was liable to burst when new wine was put into it.

The above quotation does not bring out the full meaning; the lesson is not complete without the two preceding verses. Jesus asked: 'Can friends at a wedding mourn, so long as the bridegroom is beside them?' Then he said that a piece of new cloth should not be sewn on an old coat, because it will shrink and make the tear worse. Thus, when taken together, the three verses mean that we cannot mix things that will not harmonize with each other, just as oil will not mix with water.

142   Don't put the cart before the horse
The horse pulls the cart, not the cart the horse. The proverb means that we should not get things back to front, but should deal with them in their right order. To invite all your relatives and friends to your wedding before you have arranged things with the vicar is to put the cart before the horse.

143   Don't quarrel with your bread and butter
To quarrel with your bread and butter is to give up your job without sufficient reason, which is foolish.

'Our new manager's a perfect pig!' said Janet. 'Even if I slip out for half an hour or so to do some shopping, he wants to know where I've been and why it took so long. If he doesn't change his tune I'm giving in my notice.'

'You might not get so good a position next time,' advised her friend. 'I shouldn't quarrel with my bread and butter if I were you.'

144   Don't ride the high horse
Don't give yourself airs. Don't be arrogant. Literally, a high horse is a war-horse or charger.

145   Don't speak to the man at the wheel

The driver of a car must give all his attention to his driving. If you are a passenger don't take his mind off what he is doing by talking about something else. And don't be a 'back-seat driver' by telling him what to do and what not to do. By extension this proverb means that we should never interfere with a person who is responsible for the safety of others. Our advice, however well-meant, may cause an accident.

See also IF TWO MEN RIDE ON A HORSE, ONE MUST RIDE BEHIND (329).

146   Don't take your harp to the party

Don't keep on talking about the same thing or bringing up the same subject. Literally 'to harp' is to play the harp; figuratively 'to harp on' is to dwell tediously on a matter.

Similar proverbs are HARP NOT FOR EVER ON THE SAME STRING (263); IT IS USELESS TO FLOG A DEAD HORSE (370); NOT GOOD IS IT TO HARP ON THE FRAYED STRING (515).

147   Don't teach your grandmother to suck eggs

Don't offer advice to those who are more experienced than you are. The saying is often used in the form of a retort.

'Be careful how you use that chisel. It's very sharp and may slip.'

'You go and teach your grandmother to suck eggs.'

148   Don't tell tales out of school

Don't give away any damaging secrets. Don't make public anything that should be kept private.

The proverb originated among children. To tell tales out of school was to sneak – to try to keep on good terms with the teacher by betraying other children. One of Mother Goose's Nursery Rhymes runs:

> Tell-tale-tit,
> Your tongue shall be slit,
> And all the dogs in the town
> Shall have a little bit.

A similar saying the Army is NO NAMES, NO PACK DRILL (507).

149   Don't wash your dirty linen in public
Another way of saying this is: 'Dirty linen should be washed at
home.' The meaning is that we should not discuss intimate family
matters in public, especially if they are of a shameful nature.

150   Do not wear out your welcome
This is much the same advice as A CONSTANT GUEST IS NEVER
WELCOME (91), except that it has to do with the length of stay
rather than the frequency of the visits.

151   Dog does not eat dog
This means the same as THERE IS HONOUR AMONG THIEVES (653).
On the grounds that UNITED WE STAND, DIVIDED WE FALL (707),
wrongdoers stick together in their fight against society.

See also WHEN THIEVES FALL OUT, HONEST MEN COME BY
THEIR OWN (753).

152   A door must be either shut or open
You cannot have it shut and open at the same time. You must
have one thing or the other, so make up your mind which you
want.

Other proverbs on this theme of 'either – or' are NO MAN CAN
SERVE TWO MASTERS (502); YOU CANNOT BURN THE CANDLE AT
BOTH ENDS (777); YOU CANNOT HAVE IT BOTH WAYS (781); YOU
CANNOT HAVE YOUR CAKE AND EAT IT (782); YOU CANNOT RUN
WITH THE HARE AND HUNT WITH THE HOUNDS (788); YOU
CANNOT SELL THE COW AND DRINK THE MILK (789); YOU CANNOT
SERVE GOD AND MAMMON (790).

153   A drowning man will clutch at a straw
It is said that a drowning man will clutch at even the smallest
thing to keep him afloat. Similarly a person in any desperate
position will snatch at any chance, however slender, to save himself from disaster or ruin. Often the phrase 'to clutch at a straw'
is used on its own, and in less calamitous circumstances.

'I've tried everywhere I can think of, but nobody seems to stock
spare parts for these old cars,' said Philip.

'What about that junk-dealer in Commercial Street?' suggested
his friend. 'I'm not saying it's at all likely, but he *may* have what
you want.'

'I'll shoot round and see him now!' cried Philip, clutching at a straw.

154   A dwarf on a giant's shoulders sees the farther of the two
But this is only because the height of the giant is added to his own. In the same way, if a man of little experience can add to it the greater experience of another man, he has the advantage of their combined experience.

155   Dying is as natural as living
Since all men are mortal and must die, death is as much a part of the natural order of things as life is. The implication is that we should not fear death, as it is natural and inevitable.

E

156   The early bird catches the worm
Good advice to those who get up late in the morning, or miss opportunities by not acting promptly. Of course there is the other side to it: the worm was also up early! A similar proverb is FIRST COME, FIRST SERVED (211).

157   Early to bed and early to rise . . .
>   Early to bed and early to rise,
>   Makes a man healthy, wealthy, and wise.

We owe this admirable precept to that great and versatile American, Benjamin Franklin.

158   Easier said than done
It is easier to talk about doing a thing than it is to do it. It is easier to give advice than to put it into practice.
'That tree's too close to the house. If you want more light in the rooms, why not cut it down?'
'Easier said than done. There's only one way for it to fall and I can't get the axe to it from the other side because of the wall.'
A similar proverb is DEEDS, NOT WORDS (106).

159   East or west, home is best
Wherever it is, and however far you may travel from it, THERE'S NO PLACE LIKE HOME (661).

160   Easy come, easy go
Those who get money without effort usually squander it.
   'Young Willis inherited ten thousand pounds less than two years ago, and now he hasn't a penny. Easy come, easy go.'

161   Eavesdroppers never hear any good of themselves
It doesn't do to be too curious or inquisitive.
   The projecting edges of the roof of a house are known as the 'eaves', and the space of ground on which rainwater falls from the eaves is the 'eavesdrop' – or so it used to be called in olden days. From 'eavesdrop' derived 'eavesdropper', one who stood within the eavesdrop in order to hear what was being said inside the house. It now refers to those who secretly listen to other people's conversation; and, as the proverb suggests, what they hear about themselves is usually uncomplimentary!
   Similar proverbs are THE FISH WILL SOON BE CAUGHT THAT NIBBLES AT EVERY BAIT (214); HE WHO PEEPS THROUGH A HOLE MAY SEE WHAT WILL VEX HIM (294); TOO MUCH CURIOSITY LOST PARADISE (696).

162   An empty sack cannot stand upright
The sack here is a sack of flour, from which bread is made. Just as the sack is kept upright by the flour, so is man supported and kept alive by bread.
   See also BREAD IS THE STAFF OF LIFE (60).

163   Empty vessels make the most sound
Here 'vessels' are metal receptacles such as buckets, oil-drums and petrol-cans, which, when struck, make more noise when they are empty than when they are full. The meaning of the proverb is that empty-headed persons are always the most talkative and noisy. In *The Deserted Village* Oliver Goldsmith spoke of:

> The noisy geese that gabbled o'er the pool,
> The playful children just let loose from school,
> The watch-dog's voice that bayed the whispering wind,
> And the loud laugh that spoke the vacant mind.

A similar proverb is THEY BRAG MOST WHO CAN DO THE LEAST (673). The Dutch have a saying that one penny in a money-box makes more noise than all the coins in it when it is full.

164   The end justifies the means

Dr Brewer pointed out that this implied 'that it doesn't matter what steps you take to effect your purpose, or what suffering you cause to others, so long as the purpose is a good and desirable one in itself; that you may (if, indeed, such a thing is possible) "do evil that good may come" '.

This is perhaps one of the most disputed ideas of modern times. The difference between a totalitarian government and a democratic one is mainly that the one puts complete faith in the proverb, while the other has as little to do with it as possible.

165   The end makes all equal

This means the same as DEATH IS THE GREAT LEVELLER (105).

166   An Englishman's house is his castle

He is legally entitled to his privacy. No other person may enter his house without his permission.

Here is an amusing little extract from a speech by John J. Ingalls in the United States Senate on 10th May, 1880:

'I think some orator said that though the winds of heaven might whistle around an Englishman's cottage, the King of England could not.'

See also A HEDGE BETWEEN KEEPS FRIENDSHIP GREEN (301).

167   Enough is as good as a feast

This teaches the same lesson as MODERATION IN ALL THINGS (465). We use it in such remarks as these:

'I like sopranos up to a point, but when she sang three songs straight off, her voice began to grate on me. Enough is as good as a feast, as the saying goes.'

Similar proverbs are MORE THAN ENOUGH IS TOO MUCH (472); SAFETY LIES IN THE MIDDLE COURSE (591).

168   Even a worm will turn

Metaphorically a worm is an insignificant or contemptible person. Meek and humble as he is, however, he will resist or retaliate if pushed too far.

'You wouldn't think little Percy Perkins had it in him, but on the bus this morning that cantankerous wife of his tried to pick a

quarrel with the conductor, and Percy told her in a loud voice to
shut up.'
   'Good for Percy! Even a worm will turn.'

169   Even Homer sometimes nods

Even the best of us are liable to make mistakes.
   Homer was the greatest of Greek poets. Horace, the Roman
poet, wrote of Homer's occasional poetical lapses: 'I, too, am
indignant when the worthy Homer nods, but in a long work it is
allowable to snatch a little sleep.'
   Here is an example of modern usage:
   'I've done that trip twenty times or more. I know every inch of
the road. You'd hardly believe it, but today I took a wrong turn-
ing and lost myself.'
   'These things do happen. Even Homer sometimes nods.'
   Similar proverbs are NO MAN IS INFALLIBLE (506); TO ERR IS
HUMAN (690).

170   Every ass likes to hear himself bray

The donkey (ass) is supposed to be fond of his own ugly voice. In
the same way, foolish people seem to be fond of their own voices,
since they talk too much.

171   Every cloud has a silver lining

A dark cloud that obscures the sun has brilliant edges – the silver
lining telling us that the sun is still shining in the sky. This means
that every prospect, however grim, has its consoling or hopeful
side. So don't be down-hearted!
   Similar proverbs are NEVER SAY DIE (492); NOTHING SO BAD
BUT MIGHT HAVE BEEN WORSE (520); WHILE THERE IS LIFE THERE
IS HOPE (759).

172   Every cock crows on his own dunghill

Another version of this is: 'Every cock is bold on his own dunghill.' The meaning is that anybody can boast of his courage in
safe and familiar surroundings, where his bravery is unlikely to
be put to the test.
   'Just let him call round here. I'll teach him a lesson he won't
forget in a hurry!'

173   Every dog has his day
Good fortune comes once to all of us. If I am lucky today, your turn will come later on; or, alternatively, don't be too boastful, for tomorrow our positions may be reversed.

A similar proverb is THE WORSE LUCK NOW, THE BETTER ANOTHER TIME (773).

174   Every family has a skeleton in the cupboard
Every family has a guilty secret that it does its utmost to conceal from the world. Take, for instance, the case of the widow and her three grown-up children, who came to England from Australia last year. All four are so careful about what they say that nobody imagines for a moment that they have a skeleton in the cupboard, yet the fact is that the 'widow's' husband, a criminal of the worst type, is serving life imprisonment in Brisbane.

175   Every flow must have its ebb
And every ebb has its flow. The tide goes in and out unceasingly. Our lives have similar ups and downs; neither good fortune nor ill fortune lasts for ever. To quote a radio catchphrase popular some years ago, 'What goes up must come down.'

176   Every horse thinks its own pack heaviest
We all imagine that we have a greater load to carry than anybody else; that nobody works harder than we do, or has to put up with more difficulties.

177   Every Jack must have his Jill
This consolatory proverb tells us that everyone gets a mate in the end. Jack and Jill here stand for man and woman.

178   Every law has a loophole
It is commonly thought that a clever lawyer can find a 'hole' in any law. By creeping through the hole, his client can avoid the effect of the law. In other words, the unscrupulous person can get round almost any rule or regulation to his own advantage.

179   Every little helps
This means the same as MANY A LITTLE MAKES A MICKLE (446).

180   Every man for himself, and the devil take the hindmost
This is the doctrine of self-preservation, which is said to be the

first law of nature. As the French say, 'Sauve qui peut' ('Save himself who can'). The phrase 'the devil take the hindmost' means 'bad luck on the one who is last'.

See also SELF-PRESERVATION IS THE FIRST LAW OF NATURE (596).

181   Every man has his price
Cynically, this proverb suggests that at the pinch no man is completely honourable. Provided that the bribe (price) is big enough everyone can be persuaded to act improperly.

182   Every man has the defects of his own virtues
Every good quality in a person has a correspondingly bad quality or weakness. For example, a man may be so conscientious by nature that the completion of any task he undertakes is delayed, often unnecessarily.

183   Every man is his own worst enemy
We all behave in character. The character which determines a man's behaviour is in a sense the man. So when a person does something, which we can see is bad for him, he often does it because it is his character to do so. It is therefore his character (himself) that is doing him harm and is his enemy.

184   Every medal has two sides
And so has every argument. The phrase 'the reverse of the medal' means 'the other side of the question'.

185   Every oak must be an acorn
Everything has to have a small beginning, so don't be discouraged by your own 'smallness'.

A similar proverb is GREAT OAKS FROM LITTLE ACORNS GROW (255).

186   Every why has a wherefore
There is a reason for everything.

187   Everybody's business is nobody's business
Here 'business' means 'duty' or 'task'. When nobody is directly responsible for doing a thing, nobody does it, because everybody thinks somebody else is or will be doing it.

188   Everyone to his taste

We all have our likes and dislikes. Similar proverbs are BEAUTY
IS IN THE EYE OF THE BEHOLDER (36); ONE MAN'S MEAT IS
ANOTHER MAN'S POISON (535); TASTES DIFFER (642); THERE IS
NO DISPUTING ABOUT TASTES (657).

189   Everything comes to him who waits

The person who is prepared to wait patiently usually gets what he
wants in the end, provided of course he goes on trying.

190   Everything must have a beginning

Every mighty undertaking was very small when it started. Begin-
nings are necessarily small, and everything must have a beginning.
So this is encouragement for those who have not got very far in
their careers or in any other undertaking.

191   Evil be to him who evil thinks

The French for this, *Honi soit qui mal y pense* (310), is the motto
of the Most Noble Order of the Garter, instituted by King
Edward III in about 1344. A more correct translation is 'Dis-
honour be to him who thinks evil of it' – i.e. the order. Sir Walter
Scott says in his *Essay on Chivalry* that the motto seems to apply
to possible misrepresentations that King Philip of France might
seek to make concerning the order.

192   Example is better than precept

A precept is a rule or order given to direct or instruct. 'Always
clean your teeth after meals' is a precept; it is good advice. And
it is much more likely to be followed if the giver of it sets an example and himself cleans his teeth after meals. A similar proverb
is PRACTISE WHAT YOU PREACH (563).

193   The exception proves the rule

An exception is something that does not follow the rule. When
we say that the exception proves the rule, we mean that the
excepting of some cases shows that the rule exists, or that it applies
to those not excepted. For example, it is a rule of spelling that
when the sound is like *ee* in *meet*, we use *i* before *e* except after *c*.
The only exceptions to this rule are *seize*, *weird* and *counterfeit*.
That they are exceptions prove that the rule exists and that it

applies to all other words containing the sound of *ee* in *meet*, e.g. *grief*, *niece*, *piece*.

This saying is often used as a proverb in a most illogical way: 'The only member of the team to play well was young Parfett, who was the exception that proved the rule.'

What does 'the exception that proved the rule' mean here? It means nothing at all.

194   Exchange is no robbery

This is usually the excuse given by those who have had the advantage of an unfair exchange. If Tom exchanges with Jack a pair of football boots for a camera, then complains to Jack that the camera is useless because it lets the light in, Jack can say: 'Exchange is no robbery.'

195   Expectation is better than realization

Nothing is as good as it seems beforehand. When we have gained our object, or reached the point when we can enjoy something we have been looking forward to very much, more often than not it turns out to be a disappointment. 'To travel hopefully,' wrote Robert Louis Stevenson, 'is better than to arrive, and the true success is to labour.'

See also DISTANCE LENDS ENCHANTMENT TO THE VIEW (118).

196   Experience is the mother of wisdom

Out of experience comes wisdom. We learn by our mistakes. For the meaning of 'mother' in this sense see NECESSITY IS THE MOTHER OF INVENTION (480).

197   Experience is the teacher of fools

It has been said that experience is the best teacher, but that the school fees are high. This is another way of saying that although we certainly learn by experience, we may have to pay dearly in suffering or hardship before we eventually reap the benefit. Only foolish people act in this way. Those with more intelligence are guided by that other proverb: WISE MEN LEARN BY OTHER MEN'S MISTAKES; FOOLS BY THEIR OWN (767).

198   Extremes meet

The humble man can become so humble as to be haughty about

his humbleness. In this way it might be said that the extremes of haughtiness and humbleness meet.

199   An eye for an eye, and a tooth for a tooth

This is the doctrine of revenge, preached against by Jesus Christ in his sermon on the mount:

'Ye have heard that it hath been said, An eye for an eye, and a tooth for a tooth: But I say unto you, That ye resist not evil: but whosoever shall smite thee on thy right cheek, turn to him the other also.'

See also REVENGE IS SWEET (584).

200   The eye is bigger than the belly

Many of us, particularly children, over-estimate the capacity of our stomachs.

F

201   Faint heart ne'er won fair lady

These are words of encouragement to shy suitors. They recommend boldness, for NONE BUT THE BRAVE DESERVES THE FAIR (512); and FORTUNE FAVOURS THE BOLD (224). Similar proverbs are HE WHO HESITATES IS LOST (291); NOTHING VENTURE, NOTHING HAVE (523).

202   The fairest rose is at last withered

Beauty fades and is gone. Here is a verse from *The Rubáiyát of Omar Khayyám*, translated by Edward FitzGerald:

Oh, come with old Khayyám, and leave the Wise
   To talk; one thing is certain, that Life flies;
      One thing is certain, and the Rest is Lies;
   The Flower that once has blown for ever dies.

203   Familiarity breeds contempt

Familiarity means 'close acquaintance'. In human relationships it may lead to undue intimacy, as when a master treats his servants with so much laxity that they regard themselves as his superiors rather than as his inferiors. In another sense, familiarity can cause us to look on really important things as being of no account; we know them so well and enjoy them so often that we accept them without gratitude or thankfulness. Again, if we do a thing so many times that it becomes a habit, we are liable to get careless. For example, a spiderman, one who works on high buildings in course of erection, may become so accustomed to walking along girders that familiarity breeds contempt and one day he misses his footing and falls to his death.

Other somewhat similar proverbs are DISTANCE LENDS ENCHANTMENT TO THE VIEW (118); NO MAN IS A HERO TO HIS VALET (503); A PROPHET IS NOT WITHOUT HONOUR, SAVE IN HIS OWN COUNTRY, AND IN HIS OWN HOUSE (571); RESPECT IS GREATER FROM A DISTANCE (583).

204 A fault confessed is half redressed

If you have done something wrong and admit to it, you have gone a long way towards putting things right again.

See OPEN CONFESSION IS GOOD FOR THE SOUL (544).

205 Finding's keeping

If this were taken as a general principle, it would be morally and legally wrong, but we must have a sense of proportion. To pick up a purse in the street and not hand it over to the police is dishonest, but should we come across some trifle such as a stub of pencil or a safety-pin we shall harm nobody if we slip it in our pocket saying, 'Finding's keeping.'

206 Fine feathers make fine birds

The chaffinch is much more colourful and attractive than the house sparrow, yet they are of the same family; they are both finches, and without their feathers they would be identical in appearance. Just as bright plumage gives a bird splendour – think of the peacock! – so does smart clothing make a person look more impressive than he really is.

The proverb is nearly always used in a sarcastic or ironical sense.

'Until her husband won the pools, she was the most commonplace, dowdy, illiterate creature imaginable, but now that she dresses herself up like a society queen and nearly always remembers to sound her aitches, people are already beginning to forget what she was like before.'

'Fine feathers make fine birds!'

A rather less cynical meaning of this proverb is that other people do judge us by our appearance, so we are much more likely to make a success of our lives if we dress well than if we are shabby and down-at-heel.

See also THE TAILOR MAKES THE MAN (630) and, which contradicts them both, CLOTHES DO NOT MAKE THE MAN (86).

207   Fine words butter no parsnips

This is another way of saying that ACTIONS SPEAK LOUDER THAN WORDS (3). High-flown declarations and airy promises are useless substitutes for actions.

'Darling,' said Mr Frazer to his wife, 'I think you're a wonderful manager. You run the home beautifully and your cooking is marvellous. I tell all my friends that I have a perfect wife, economical and able to make do, and not half so extravagant as other wives.'

Mrs Frazer had heard all this before.

'Fine words butter no parsnips,' she said. 'What about giving me the housekeeping money?'

Similar proverbs are DEEDS, NOT WORDS (106); THE GREATEST TALKERS ARE THE LEAST DOERS (256); HE WHO GIVES FAIR WORDS FEEDS YOU WITH AN EMPTY SPOON (288); A LITTLE HELP IS WORTH A DEAL OF PITY (416); PRAISE WITHOUT PROFIT PUTS LITTLE IN THE POT (565).

208   Fingers were made before forks

Man used his fingers for eating before forks were invented. The proverb is quoted as an excuse for eating anything in one's fingers instead of using a fork.

209   The first blow is half the battle

Whoever gets his blow in first catches his adversary at a disadvantage. Here, for the sake of example, is a description of a football match:

'The home team scored a goal within two minutes of the start of the game, which so discouraged the visitors that they lost all confidence in themselves and were soundly beaten by ten goals to nothing.'

210   First catch your hare

You cannot cook and eat it until you have caught it, which may not be easy. Don't decide what you are going to do with a thing until it is in your possession. Act prudently and don't be over-optimistic.

Similar proverbs are CATCH YOUR BEAR BEFORE YOU SELL ITS SKIN (76); DON'T COUNT YOUR CHICKENS BEFORE THEY ARE HATCHED (124); DO NOT HALLOO TILL YOU ARE OUT OF THE WOOD (131); NEVER SPEND YOUR MONEY BEFORE YOU HAVE IT (493); THERE'S MANY A SLIP 'TWIXT THE CUP AND THE LIP (655).

211   First come, first served
This is the penalty of lateness. Those who arrive early get a better choice.

'I bought a lovely dress for two pounds at the sale,' Mary told her friend.

'Lucky you,' said Beryl. 'All the best bargains had gone before I got there. Still, I mustn't grumble, I suppose. First come, first served.'

A similar proverb is THE EARLY BIRD CATCHES THE WORM (156).

212   First impressions are most lasting
We may have met a person many times since our first meeting, but his or her appearance as it struck us then is the one that lingers longest in our minds.

213   First thrive and then wive
The wording is old but the lesson is as fresh as ever. Don't marry until you can well afford to do so.

See also WHEN THE WOLF COMES IN AT THE DOOR, LOVE CREEPS OUT OF THE WINDOW (751).

214   The fish will soon be caught that nibbles at every bait
It doesn't do to be too curious or inquisitive. Similar proverbs are EAVESDROPPERS NEVER HEAR ANY GOOD OF THEMSELVES (161); HE WHO PEEPS THROUGH A HOLE MAY SEE WHAT WILL VEX HIM (294); TOO MUCH CURIOSITY LOST PARADISE (696).

215   Fling dirt enough and some will stick
Tell enough lies about a person and some of them will be believed. In the modern way of speaking, the process is known as a 'smear campaign'.

'I don't care what they say about me. It isn't true, so why should
I worry?'

'Don't forget the old proverb: "Fling dirt enough and some will
stick." '

Similar proverbs are GIVE A DOG A BAD NAME AND HANG HIM
(230); GIVE A LIE TWENTY-FOUR HOURS' START, AND YOU CAN
NEVER OVERTAKE IT (231).

216   A fool and his money are soon parted

This is a similar proverb to EASY COME, EASY GO (160). A wise
man spends his money prudently; a foolish man spends his without thought and is soon penniless. He is 'parted' from his money.

While the collection box was being passed round at Sunday
School, the teacher said encouragingly:

'It is better to give than to take. How true these old proverbs
still are, aren't they, children?'

'Yes, miss,' agreed young Tommy Green with feeling as he put
in his penny. 'A fool and his money are soon parted.'

217   Fools rush in where angels fear to tread

Foolish people act hastily and do or say things that wiser people
would avoid. Angels here represent people of wisdom. The proverb is a line from Pope's *Essay on Criticism* (1711).

218   Footprints on the sands of time are not made by sitting down

This refers to the seventh stanza of Longfellow's *A Psalm of Life*:

> Lives of great men all remind us
> We can make our lives sublime,
> And, departing, leave behind us
> Footprints on the sands of time.

'Footprints on the sands of time' are the things by which – or
for which – we are remembered by those who come after us.
Napoleon wrote in a letter: 'We should endeavour to do something so that we may say that we have not lived in vain, that we
may leave some mark of ourselves on the sands of time.'

But not the mark we make when we sit down!

219   For want of a nail . . .

For want of a nail the shoe is lost, for want of a shoe the horse is
lost, for want of a horse the rider is lost.

This proverb, which stresses the importance of seeming trifles, dates back to the seventeenth century. In the eighteenth century Benjamin Franklin expanded it as follows:

> For the want of a nail the shoe was lost,
> For the want of a shoe the horse was lost,
> For the want of a horse the rider was lost,
> For the want of a rider the battle was lost,
> For the want of a battle the kingdom was lost—
> And all for the want of a horshoe-nail.

220 Forbidden fruit is sweetest

If we are told that we must not have a thing, we want it more than ever; and if we are told not to do a thing, we feel impelled to do it.

A schoolboy once came upon a form-mate smoking in a quiet corner behind the gymnasium.

'Are you enjoying it, Jenkins?' he asked.

'Not very much,' admitted Jenkins, 'but the ban on smoking makes it more exciting.'

The proverb derives, of course, from the story of Adam and Eve in the Book of Genesis. See TOO MUCH CURIOSITY LOST PARADISE (696).

221 A forced kindness deserves no thanks

No doubt the doer of the kindness is thanked, but he does not deserve to be if he has done it against his will – or to further his own ends.

222 Forewarned is forearmed

If we are warned beforehand that something is going to happen we are able to take all necessary steps in advance.

'A little bird has told me,' said the works manager, 'that the factory inspector is visiting us on Thursday, which gives us a chance to make sure the guards and lifting gear are all O.K. before he arrives. They're very hot on these safety regulations, and I hate being taken by surprise.'

'Forewarned,' grinned the foreman, 'is forearmed.'

223 Forgive and forget

This means the same as LET BYGONES BE BYGONES (393).

224 Fortune favours the bold

The successful people in life are those who have the courage to try. The lesson the proverb teaches can be given in three words: 'Have a go!'

See also FAINT HEART NE'ER WON FAIR LADY (201); NOTHING VENTURE, NOTHING HAVE (523).

225 Fortune knocks at least once at every man's gate

Opportunity comes to everyone at least once, and when it does come we should seize it, for OPPORTUNITY SELDOM KNOCKS TWICE (546).

226 A friend in need is a friend indeed

Your real friends are those who remain your friends when you are really in need of help.

A similar proverb is PROSPERITY MAKES FRIENDS, ADVERSITY TRIES THEM (572).

227 From the sublime to the ridiculous is but a step

This is an English translation of Napoleon's famous remark after the retreat from Moscow in 1812. We use it when anyone in an important position, or on an important occasion, is made to look foolish by some sudden mishap that causes amusement to everybody except himself.

228 Full of courtesy, full of craft

Beware of a man who is too extravagantly polite, for he is probably trying to cheat you.

See also MANY KISS THE HAND THEY WISH TO CUT OFF (448).

G

229 Gather ye rosebuds while ye may

Take advantage of your opportunities before it is too late, for LIFE IS SHORT AND TIME IS SWIFT (404). The proverb comes from Robert Herrick's poem *To the Virgins, to make Much of Time.* Here are the first and last of the four stanzas:

> Gather ye rosebuds while ye may,
>   Old Time is still a-flying:
> And this same flower that smiles to-day
>   To-morrow will be dying.

> Then be not coy, but use your time;
> And while ye may, go marry:
> For having lost but once your prime,
> You may for ever tarry.

A similar proverb is MAKE HAY WHILE THE SUN SHINES (436) Other proverbs on the theme of opportunity are listed under OPPORTUNITY SELDOM KNOCKS TWICE (546).

230   Give a dog a bad name and hang him
This is much the same as FLING DIRT ENOUGH AND SOME WILL STICK (215). The phrase 'a bad name' means 'a bad reputation'. However untrue the charges may be, they may ruin a man's reputation and so 'hang him' – that is, end all chance of his ever re-establishing himself as an honest and respectable citizen.

231   Give a lie twenty-four hours' start, and you can never overtake it
If a lie is not refuted immediately, it will pass from mouth to mouth until it is accepted as truth by everybody. See also FLING DIRT ENOUGH AND SOME WILL STICK (215); GIVE A DOG A BAD NAME AND HANG HIM (230).

232   Give a thief enough rope and he'll hang himself
If you give a bad person enough opportunities he will bring about his own downfall.

There is a play on words in this proverb, for 'rope' has two meanings: (a) a length of stout cordage as used for hanging, which was the penalty for theft in olden days; and (b) liberty of action. We can appreciate the second meaning when we consider a tethered goat, which a long rope allows to feed on a larger area of grass than does a short one. Hence we can reword the old proverb thus: 'Give a thief enough chances to steal and he will become so over-confident that he will get himself into jail.'

Figuratively the proverb can be used as follows:

'That new member,' said the secretary of the Golf Club, 'has already offended several other members with his rudeness. We can't very well ask him to resign so soon, can we?'

'I suggest letting things take their course,' was the reply. 'Give him enough rope and he'll hang himself. When he's offended the whole Club and nobody will play with him, he'll *have* to resign.'

233   Give and take
Be as ready to give as to take; to help others as you are to be helped; to make concessions as to accept them; to listen to other people's views as to give them yours. Life is a two-way process. Without give and take we cannot live in harmony together.
See also ONE GOOD TURN DESERVES ANOTHER (531).

234   Give credit where credit is due
Here 'credit' means 'acknowledgement of merit' and has nothing to do with money. The proverb means that we should acknowledge the good points of even those we dislike or disapprove of.
'Mark you, I can't stand the fellow, but I'll give him credit for his business efficiency.'
See also THE DEVIL IS NOT SO BLACK AS HE IS PAINTED (112) and GIVE THE DEVIL HIS DUE (236).

235   Give knaves an inch and they will take a yard
If you grant some people a small favour, it only encourages them to take much more than they are offered.
'I told old Joe to help himself to some strawberries, and when I went out into the garden later in the morning, I found he'd pinched the lot.'
'Never trust old Joe. Give him an inch and he'll take a yard.'

236   Give the devil his due
Even the very bad sometimes do a good deed, so we should recognize the good points of others, even though they are not friends of ours.
See also THE DEVIL IS NOT SO BLACK AS HE IS PAINTED (112) and GIVE CREDIT WHERE CREDIT IS DUE (234).

237   Give us the tools, and we will finish the job
Winston Churchill said this to the Americans in a broadcast address on 9th February, 1941. The tools were the means by which we could carry on and win World War II.
See also YOU CANNOT MAKE BRICKS WITHOUT STRAW (786).

238   Gluttony kills more than the sword
More people die from overeating than are slain in battle. This is a very old proverb, dating back to the times when gluttony was

more common than it is today, and it was no rare thing for people to die of a surfeit of this or that (King Henry I is reported to have died of a surfeit of lampreys). Of course, in many cases the real cause may have been ptomaine poisoning, arising from the quality rather than the quantity of the food eaten, but for all that, this is not a bad motto for those who want to lose weight.

239   God helps those who help themselves
If you want to succeed you must make the effort yourself.

That eminent Spanish writer, Miguel de Unamuno, put it this way: ' "Let God do all," someone will say; but if man folds his arms, God will go to sleep.' This brings to mind the story of the new vicar who paused to pass the time of day with old Amos, who was weeding his flower-beds.

'What a beautiful garden you have made with God's help,' said the vicar.

Amos chuckled as he replied: 'You should 'ave seen it when the Almighty 'ad it all to 'imself!'

240   God is always on the side of the big battalions
In most wars both sides claim the support of the Almighty, yet victory invariably goes to the stronger. An alternative version is PROVIDENCE IS ALWAYS ON THE SIDE OF THE BIG BATTALIONS. See also MIGHT IS RIGHT (460).

241   God made the country, and man made the town
This has general application and means that natural scenery (God-made) is better than man-made objects.

242   God tempers the wind to the shorn lamb
Here 'tempers' means 'softens, makes less severe', and 'shorn' means 'with its wool cut off'. The proverb means that God treats the weak with greater kindness than he shows to those better able to look after themselves. In his *A Sentimental Journey through France and Italy*, Laurence Sterne tells of his second meeting with Maria, a girl who had lost her reason. Since last they had met she had travelled much – alone across the Apennines, over all Lombardy without money, and through the flinty roads of Savoy without shoes. 'How she had borne it, and how she had got supported, she could not tell, but, "God tempers the wind," said Maria, "to the shorn lamb." '

243   The gods send nuts to those who have no teeth
In this life we either have too little of what we do want, or too much of what we don't want or can't use. WATER IS A BOON IN THE DESERT, BUT THE DROWNING MAN CURSES IT (717).

244   The golden age was never the present age
A golden age is the most prosperous period of a nation's condition or literature. It is to be noted, however, that it is always in the past; those who lived during it probably did not realize how fortunate they were, and looked forward to better times! It was a case of JAM TOMORROW AND JAM YESTERDAY – BUT NEVER JAM TODAY (377).

245   A golden key opens every door
The 'golden key' is money, which overcomes for its possessors all the obstacles barring the way to poorer folk. See also MONEY TALKS (469).

246   Good company on the road is the shortest cut
A journey on foot seems much longer when we make it alone than when we do it with pleasant companions.

247   Good fences make good neighbours
This means the same as A HEDGE BETWEEN KEEPS FRIENDSHIP GREEN (301).

248   A good husband makes a good wife
A husband who treats his wife well is likely to be treated well in return. In its more general application this means that everyone responds to good treatment by his fellows.

249   A good name is sooner lost than won
It takes a long time to build up a good reputation, but this reputation is quickly lost by just one crime or piece of bad behaviour.

250   A good tale is none the worse for being told twice
Children, in particular, love to hear a story again, however many times they have heard it before. 'Mummy, please tell me the story of the girl who had two wicked sisters, who went out and left her

to do all the housework, and one day a fairy turns a pumpkin into a beautiful coach and she goes to the ball in it, and the prince falls in love with her and they get married. Do tell me that one, Mummy.'

251   Good wine needs no bush
High-quality goods need no advertising because people soon get to know about them.

In olden days, taverns and private houses where beer or wine could be bought by travellers had a branch or bunch of ivy hung up outside, ivy being sacred to Bacchus, the god of wine in Greek mythology. If the liquor offered for sale was of excellent quality, there was no lack of customers, so there was no need to hang out the ivy.

252   The grapes are sour
People who cannot get what they want are inclined to pretend that they never wanted it, in order to save face. This comes from the fable of the fox that tried hard to reach a bunch of grapes, but failed. He then said they were certainly unripe, so that he was able to go away satisfied.

253   Grasp all, lose all
Don't be avaricious. If you are too greedy you will lose even what you have already. The dog in the fable was carrying a piece of meat across a bridge. He glanced down into the water and saw what he took to be another dog with a piece of meat in its mouth. He opened his jaws to snatch at the meat in the reflection – and his own piece fell into the water.

254   A great city, a great solitude
Sometimes 'loneliness' is used instead of 'solitude'. The saying comes to us from the Greek. It means that in a large centre of civilization, where many thousands of people are going about their own affairs and are not interested in anyone else, we can feel as lonely as if we were on a desert island.

255   Great oaks from little acorns grow
Everything has to have a small beginning, so don't be discouraged by your own 'smallness'. Here is an example of the way in which the proverb is used:

'He set up in business fifty years ago in a tiny, poky shop in the East End of London, and now the company he founded has branches all over the country.'

'Great oaks from little acorns grow.'

256 The greatest talkers are the least doers
Those who talk the most do less than anybody else. This proverb means much the same as ACTIONS SPEAK LOUDER THAN WORDS (3) and EMPTY VESSELS MAKE THE MOST SOUND (163).

257 A growing youth has a wolf in his belly
He is always hungry.

H

258 Half a loaf is better than no bread
We should be thankful for what we receive, even though it is not so much as we had hoped for.

'I applied for a fortnight's holiday, but we're so short-handed that they'd only give me a week. Still, half a loaf's better than no bread.'

A somewhat similar proverb is ANY PORT IN A STORM (18).

259 Half the world knows not how the other half lives
People of one social class are often ignorant of the problems of those of another class. This was even truer formerly than now, so it is not surprising to find the proverb in English literature as early as 1640 (Herbert) and in French as early as 1532 (Rabelais).

260 The hand that rocks the cradle rules the world
Mothers who look after their children are bringing up a new generation of men. The following lines were written by William Ross Wallace:

> They say that man is mighty,
>   He governs land and sea,
> He wields a mighty sceptre
>   O'er lesser powers that be;
> But a mightier power and stronger
>   Man from his throne has hurled,
> For the hand that rocks the cradle
>   Is the hand that rules the world.

261 Handsome is as handsome does
Good living is more important than good looks. 'Handsome' means not only 'good-looking, of fine appearance', but also 'generous'.

'He always treats me very well, but there's no denying he's an ugly old devil.'

'Never mind about that. Handsome is as handsome does.'

262 Happy is the country that has no history
Often 'nation' is used instead of 'country'. Edward Gibbon wrote in *The Decline and Fall of the Roman Empire*: 'History is, indeed, little more than the register of the crimes, follies, and misfortunes of mankind.' Thomas Jefferson wrote: 'Blest is that Nation whose silent course of happiness furnishes nothing for history to say.'

263 Harp not for ever on the same string
Don't keep on talking about the same thing or bringing up the same subject. Literally 'to harp' is to play the harp; figuratively 'to harp on' is to dwell tediously on a matter.

Similar proverbs are DON'T TAKE YOUR HARP TO THE PARTY (146); IT IS USELESS TO FLOG A DEAD HORSE (370); NOT GOOD IS IT TO HARP ON THE FRAYED STRING (515).

264 Haste makes waste
The more hurry we are in, the more likely we are to drop an egg on the floor or spill the milk.

'Haste makes waste', runs the old saying, 'and waste makes want, and want makes strife between the good man and his wife'. The term 'good man' meant the head of the household.

A similar proverb is MORE HASTE, LESS SPEED (470).

265 Haste trips over its own heels
This also means the same as MORE HASTE, LESS SPEED (470).

266 He cannot speak well that cannot hold his tongue
This teaches the value of silence at times when to speak would do more harm than good. Similar proverbs are: SPEECH IS SILVER, SILENCE IS GOLDEN (613); THERE IS A TIME TO SPEAK AND A TIME TO BE SILENT (652).

267   He gives twice who gives quickly
The person who gives immediately is twice as helpful as the one who gives too late. The proverb is a translation of the Latin *Bis dat qui cito dat*.

268   He is rich that has few wants
A person who has few wants can easily satisfy them. In this sense he is 'richer' than the rich man who has many wants that he cannot satisfy.

269   He laughs best who laughs last
You may not come off best in the end, so don't laugh too soon. The following little incident is borrowed from *Three Men in a Boat* by Jerome K. Jerome. The narrator has just had an early-morning dip in the Thames.

I was very cold when I got back into the boat, and, in my hurry to get my shirt on, I accidentally jerked it into the water. It made me awfully wild, especially as George burst out laughing. I could not see anything to laugh at, and I told George so, and he only laughed the more. I never saw a man laugh so much. I quite lost my temper with him at last, and I pointed out to him what a drivelling maniac of an imbecile idiot he was; but he only roared the louder. And then, just as I was landing the shirt, I noticed that it was not my shirt at all, but George's, which I had mistaken for mine; whereupon the humour of the thing struck me for the first time, and *I* began to laugh. And the more I looked from George's wet shirt to George, roaring with laughter, the more I was amused, and I laughed so much that I had to let the shirt fall back into the water again.

'Aren't you – you – going to get it out?' said George between his shrieks.

I could not answer him for a while, I was laughing so, but at last, between my peals I managed to jerk out:

'It isn't my shirt – it's *yours*!'

I never saw a man's face change from lively to severe so suddenly in all my life before. I tried to make him see the fun of the thing, but he could not. George is very dense at seeing a joke sometimes.

He laughs best who laughs last.

270   He should have a long spoon that sups with the devil
Anyone who mixes with evil companions must have all his wits about him.

Other proverbs dealing with the dangers of keeping bad company are HE THAT TOUCHETH PITCH SHALL BE DEFILED (279); THE ROTTEN APPLE INJURES ITS NEIGHBOURS (590); WHO KEEPS COMPANY WITH THE WOLF WILL LEARN TO HOWL (762).

271 He that cannot obey cannot command
We must learn to obey orders before we are qualified to give them. The experience gained in a subordinate position is invaluable when we have to take charge.

Similar proverbs are IT NEEDS MORE SKILL THAN I CAN TELL TO PLAY THE SECOND FIDDLE WELL (371); THROUGH OBEDIENCE LEARN TO COMMAND (683).

272 He that commits a fault thinks everyone speaks of it
When you have done something wrong you are so conscious of it that you feel that everyone else knows about it.

A similar proverb is CONSCIENCE DOES MAKE COWARDS OF US ALL (89).

273 He that fights and runs away may live to fight another day
Although a brave man is better than a coward, caution is often better than rashness.

A similar proverb is DISCRETION IS THE BETTER PART OF VALOUR (117).

274 He that has a great nose thinks everybody is speaking of it
Don't be self-conscious. Don't be embarrassed if you have a big nose, or your ears stick out, or you need a hair-do, or you didn't clean your shoes this morning. You yourself are much more likely to be conscious of these things than anyone else is.

275 He that hath a full purse never wanted a friend
Here 'wanted' means 'lacked'. A similar proverb is SUCCESS HAS MANY FRIENDS (626). Because a man is rich, he is always surrounded by flatterers and yes-men. For the same reason, A RICH MAN'S JOKE IS ALWAYS FUNNY (585).

276 He that hath not silver in his purse should have silk in his tongue
A man without money cannot afford to offend those to whom he looks for financial assistance.

277 He that hath wife and children hath given hostages to fortune
A man with a wife and family cannot be so adventurous, or take
so many chances, as an unmarried man. A hostage is a person given
to another as a pledge or security. 'Hostages to fortune' are persons or things that one may lose.

The proverb comes from Francis Bacon's essay, *Of Marriage
and Single Life*: 'He that hath wife and children hath given hostages to fortune; for they are impediments to great enterprises,
either of virtue or mischief.'

A similar proverb is HE TRAVELS THE FASTEST WHO TRAVELS
ALONE (284). See also WEDLOCK IS A PADLOCK (722).

278 He that is down need fear no fall
A person who occupies the lowest position in life cannot fall any
further and therefore has no fear of falling, whereas the great
constantly fear the possibility of their downfall. The proverb is
also quoted to console those who have just met with failure and
have 'fallen' in that sense.

279 He that toucheth pitch shall be defiled
This comes from the Apocrypha and is a warning against mixing
with the rich. 'As the wild ass is the lion's prey in the wilderness,
so the rich eat up the poor.' In general it is a warning against
wickedness. Keep company with evil men and soon you will be
'tarred with the same brush' – no more virtuous than they.

Other proverbs dealing with the dangers of keeping bad company are HE SHOULD HAVE A LONG SPOON THAT SUPS WITH THE
DEVIL (270); THE ROTTEN APPLE INJURES ITS NEIGHBOURS (590);
WHO KEEPS COMPANY WITH THE WOLF WILL LEARN TO HOWL
(762).

280 He that will not when he may, when he will he shall have nay
Here 'nay' means 'a refusal'. This proverb could apply to a certain Mr Lambert. One afternoon he was telephoned by a friend
who offered him a free ticket for the theatre that evening. Mr
Lambert did not want to go, so he declined with thanks. Half an
hour later he changed his mind and rang his friend back, only to
be told that the ticket had been given to somebody else.

A similar proverb is OPPORTUNITY SELDOM KNOCKS TWICE
(546).

281 He that would eat the kernel must crack the nut
You cannot eat an almond without first cracking the shell. By extension, you cannot expect to get anything without working for it.

282 He that would have eggs must endure the cackling of hens
To enjoy one thing, you must be prepared to put up with another. TAKE THE ROUGH WITH THE SMOOTH (635).

283 He that would the daughter win, must with the mother first begin
Most mothers exercise a considerable influence over their daughters, so to gain the goodwill of the mother is an important step towards marrying the daughter.

284 He travels the fastest who travels alone
An ambitious man can get along much better when he is not hampered by a wife and family, or by friends who hold him back. The quotation comes from Rudyard Kipling's poem, *The Winners*, which he describes as a 'heretical song'. Here is part of the first verse:

> A friend at a pinch is a friend indeed,
> But a fool to wait for the laggard behind.
> Down to Gehenna or up to the Throne,
> He travels the fastest who travels alone.

See also HE THAT HATH WIFE AND CHILDREN HATH GIVEN HOSTAGES TO FORTUNE (277).

285 He who begins many things, finishes but few
Many of us lack the power to concentrate. We start on something, but soon tire of it and transfer our interest to something else. The result is that we seldom complete what we have undertaken.
A similar proverb is DON'T HAVE TOO MANY IRONS IN THE FIRE (132).

286 He who denies all confesses all
If a person has something he wishes to conceal, he can be so persistent in his expressions of innocence that his hearers become convinced that he is lying.

287 He who excuses himself accuses himself
We suspect the person who makes too many excuses, because he

is probably covering up his ill actions. It is better to admit a thing frankly than to make excuses, for the excuses are such obvious evasions that they irritate instead of convincing.

288 He who gives fair words feeds you with an empty spoon
We gain nothing from being flattered; nor do we profit from other people's excuses.

Similar proverbs are FINE WORDS BUTTER NO PARSNIPS (207); PRAISE WITHOUT PROFIT PUTS LITTLE IN THE POT (565).

289 He who goes against the fashion is himself its slave
This paradox was coined by Logan Pearsall Smith, the essayist. Fashion can here be defined as 'a prevailing custom, especially in dress'. It has been said that we are all slaves to it, yet there are always those who refuse to conform and deliberately go against it. Fashion, however, is constantly changing, with the result that these upholders of personal freedom have to alter their costume accordingly, which makes them also fashion's slaves.

In a wider sense, anyone who 'kicks against the pricks' is adding to the difficulties of his existence. A man who takes up a life of crime because he dislikes work of any kind often works much harder than those in honest employment.

290 He who handles a nettle tenderly is soonest stung
Face danger boldly and it won't hurt you. As the old rhyme has it:

> Tender-handed stroke a nettle,
>   And it stings you for your pains;
> Grasp it like a man of mettle,
>   And it soft as silk remains.

Harry Hotspur says in Shakespeare's *Henry IV* (Part I): 'Out of this nettle, danger, we pluck this flower, safety.'

A similar proverb is THE BULL MUST BE TAKEN BY THE HORNS (62).

291 He who hesitates is lost
This applies to any situation where an opportunity is lost through failure to make up one's mind. See also LOOK BEFORE YOU LEAP (426).

Other proverbs on the theme of opportunity are listed under OPPORTUNITY SELDOM KNOCKS TWICE (546).

292   He who makes no mistakes makes nothing
The person who is so careful that he never makes a mistake is unlikely to achieve anything of real value.

293   He who pays the piper calls the tune
In olden days music for dancing on the village green and in other rural surroundings was provided by strolling musicians. Of course these pipers did not perform for nothing, and who ever paid for their services had the right to tell them which tunes to play. By extension the proverb means that a person who puts up the money for anything has a say in how the money is to be expended.
  'Well, he gave the Cricket Club thirty-five pounds for a new motor-mower, so I don't see how we can spend it on cricket caps and Club ties. Don't forget that he who pays the piper calls the tune.'

294   He who peeps through a hole may see what will vex him
It doesn't do to be too curious or inquisitive. Similar proverbs are EAVESDROPPERS NEVER HEAR ANY GOOD OF THEMSELVES (161); THE FISH WILL SOON BE CAUGHT THAT NIBBLES AT EVERY BAIT (214); TOO MUCH CURIOSITY LOST PARADISE (696).

295   He who rides a tiger is afraid to dismount
Whatever the discomfort of his present condition – for nobody really favours this means of transport – it is better than dismounting and being eaten by the tiger. A similar predicament is to have a wolf by the ears; one cannot continue holding on indefinitely, yet dare not let go. In a figurative sense, a man can be said to be riding a tiger when he is compelled to go on doing what he is doing because of what may happen when he stops. For example, a manager who has been defrauding his employers cannot take a holiday for fear that his dishonesty will be discovered while he is away.

296   He who says what he likes shall hear what he does not like
A man who claims that he always speaks his mind does not expect others to do the same, and is annoyed when they give him a dose of his own medicine – that is, treat him as he treats them. As was once remarked on this matter of free speech: 'You are forthright and outspoken. The other chap is just naturally rude.'

297 He who would climb the ladder must begin at the bottom
There are no short cuts in the climbing of a ladder; one can reach the top only by going up rung by rung. In a figurative sense a ladder is a means of rising in the world or attaining one's object, and here again the ascent is not rapid but in stages. A young man cannot become chairman of the company overnight; he must start as a junior clerk and work his way up step by step.

We speak also of 'getting a foot on the ladder of success'. This means 'getting a first opportunity to rise to fame', e.g. 'He got his foot on the ladder of success when he was given the part of Romeo at the New Theatre in 1935.'

298 Health is better than wealth
It is better to be healthy than rich, since ill-health makes a person unhappy, even though he is rich. This is a consolation to the poor, who can very likely achieve good health as easily as the rich can.

299 Heaven helps those who help themselves
Another version of GOD HELPS THOSE WHO HELP THEMSELVES (239).

300 A heavy purse makes a light heart
We can afford to be cheerful when we have no money troubles. The reverse, of course, is A LIGHT PURSE MAKES A HEAVY HEART (407).

301 A hedge between keeps friendship green
We remain better friends if we do not see too much of one another. Our neighbour does not live in our house and we do not live in his. Hedges or fences between our properties are not just physical barriers; they are a reminder to both of us that a good neighbour should never be obtrusive.

Similar proverbs are GOOD FENCES MAKE GOOD NEIGHBOURS (247); LOVE YOUR NEIGHBOUR, YET PULL NOT DOWN YOUR FENCE (434). Akin to these is AN ENGLISHMAN'S HOUSE IS HIS CASTLE (166).

302 Help a lame dog over a stile
Give assistance to anyone in difficulties or distress.

303 Hew not too high lest the chips fall in thine eye
Don't be too ambitious. Realize your own limitations. Like the man who tries to use an axe above his head instead of at a level low enough for him to use it effectively, if you try to live above your proper station in life you are liable to suffer humiliation. On the other hand, FAINT HEART NE'ER WON FAIR LADY (201).

304 Hide not your light under a bushel
Don't be too modest to set others a good example.
Here a bushel is a measure, a container for corn, etc. The source of the proverb is Matthew, v, 15. During the sermon on the mount Jesus said to his disciples: 'Ye are the light of the world. A city that is set on an hill cannot be hid. Neither do men light a candle, and put it under a bushel, but on a candlestick; and it giveth light to all that are in the house. Let your light so shine before men, that they may see your good works, and glorify your Father which is in heaven.'
A similar proverb is WHAT IS THE GOOD OF A SUNDIAL IN THE SHADE? (731).

305 The highest branch is not the safest roost
This is the penalty of greatness. When a man is at the top of his profession he is said to be 'at the top of the tree'. In consequence he has farther to fall than those below him, all of whom are equally anxious to get to the highest branch.
See also UNEASY LIES THE HEAD THAT WEARS A CROWN (706).

306 History repeats itself
What has happened once is liable to happen again. The phrase derives from the works of Thucydides, the Greek historian. 'I shall be content,' he wrote, 'if those shall pronounce my History useful who desire to give a view of events as they really happened, and as they are very likely, in accordance with human nature, to repeat themselves at some future time – if not exactly the same, yet very similar.'

307 Hitch your wagon to a star
Have high ideals. Make it your aim to rise above worldly things.
We owe the proverb to Ralph Waldo Emerson, the American philosopher. Here is a condensed version of what he wrote:

Everything good in man leans on what is higher. All our strength and success in the work of our hands depend on our borrowing the aid of the elements . . . I admire the skill which, on the sea-shore, makes the tides drive wheels and grind corn, and which thus engages the assistance of the moon, like a hired hand. Now that is the wisdom of a man, in every instance of his labor, to hitch his wagon to a star, and see his chore done by the gods themselves . . . Hitch your wagon to a star. Let us not flag in paltry works which serve our pot and bag alone . . . Work rather for those interests which the divinities honor and promote – justice, love, freedom, knowledge, utility.

308   Hoist your sail when the wind is fair
Don't act when circumstances are unfavourable. Wait for a better opportunity of achieving success – and when it comes, seize upon it.

Other proverbs on this theme are listed under OPPORTUNITY SELDOM KNOCKS TWICE (546).

309   Honesty is the best policy
Here 'policy' means 'course of action'. If we have to decide on a course of action, honesty is the best one to follow. It is not a question of morals alone, but of wise choice. Although dishonesty may prove profitable for a while, honesty pays in the long run.

310   Honi soit qui mal y pense
This is one of those proverbs that have remained more common in their original form than in the English translation. It is the French for EVIL BE TO HIM WHO EVIL THINKS (191).

311   Hope deferred maketh the heart sick
When we have to wait indefinitely for our hopes to be realized, we become sad and disillusioned.

The full saying is to be found in Proverbs, xiii, 12: 'Hope deferred maketh the heart sick: but when the desire cometh, it is a tree of life.' In his translation of the Bible, James Moffatt made the meaning clear to this generation of ours by rendering it thus: 'Hope deferred is sickening: it is new life to have desire fulfilled.'

312   Hope for the best and prepare for the worst
We should all be optimistic, but ready at the same time to meet trouble and difficulties whenever they arise. For instance, an Amateur Dramatic Society who are hoping to present *A Midsummer Night's Dream* in the open air should prepare for the

worst by arranging for the performance to be given under cover in the event of bad weather.

313 Hope springs eternal in the human breast
It is in the nature of man to look forward to better times, despite set-backs and disappointments.

The proverb is a quotation from Pope's *Essay on Man* (1733):

> Hope springs eternal in the human breast:
> Man never is, but always to be, blest.
> The soul, uneasy and confin'd from home,
> Rests and expatiates in a life to come.

The second line means that man never is blissfully happy, yet always thinks he is about to be. In the fourth line 'expatiates' means 'wanders freely'.

Other proverbs on the theme of hope are EVERY CLOUD HAS A SILVER LINING (171); NEVER SAY DIE (492); WHILE THERE IS LIFE THERE IS HOPE (759).

314 A house divided against itself cannot stand
Discord breaks up families. The source of the proverb is Mark, iii, 25, 'house' meaning 'household'.

A similar proverb is UNITED WE STAND, DIVIDED WE FALL (707).

315 Hunger is the best sauce
Nothing gives us an appetite like hunger. We do not need sauce or other relish to add flavour to even the plainest of food when we are really hungry.

316 Hypocrisy is a homage that vice pays to virtue
Even the worst sinners value the good opinions of their fellow men. To gain those good opinions they try to hide their real natures by acting as though they are persons of good repute – and that is hypocrisy.

I

317 Idle folk have the least leisure
People who are lazy by nature are so reluctant to take on work that they give the impression of having no spare time. In addition, they spend so much effort avoiding work that they in fact use up their leisure time.

On the other hand BUSIEST MEN FIND THE MOST TIME (66).

318　If a man deceives me once, shame on him; if he deceives me twice, shame on me

If I am foolish enough to allow him to deceive me on one occasion, I have only myself to blame if I let him do it again.

A similar proverb is ONCE BITTEN, TWICE SHY (526).

319　If a thing is worth doing it is worth doing well

If what you propose to do deserves your attention, and is not so trivial that time should not be wasted on it, do it to the best of your ability.

It was G. K. Chesterton who invented the paradox: 'If a thing is worth doing it is worth doing badly.' In other words, if a thing is worth doing it is worth making an attempt at it, rather than not trying at all.

A similar proverb is NEVER DO THINGS BY HALVES (486). See also THE BEST IS OFTEN THE ENEMY OF THE GOOD (40).

320　If at first you don't succeed, try, try, try again

This teaches patience and perseverance. Don't be down-hearted. Don't let early failures deter you from your purpose. Stick to it and you will finally succeed.

Other proverbs on this theme are CONSTANT DRIPPING WEARS AWAY THE STONE (90); IT'S DOGGED THAT DOES IT (356); LITTLE BY LITTLE AND BIT BY BIT (415); LITTLE STROKES FELL GREAT OAKS (419); ROME WAS NOT BUILT IN A DAY (588); SLOW BUT SURE WINS THE RACE (603); WHERE THERE'S A WILL THERE'S A WAY (755).

321　If each would sweep before his own door, we should have a clean city

This had a literal meaning in the days when householders got rid of their refuse by throwing it out into the street. A figurative meaning, suited to the present time, is that the welfare of society as a whole depends on the individual behaviour of those that make it up.

322　If 'ifs' and 'ans' were pots and pans . . .

If we could achieve our aims by merely wishing, life would be very easy.

The archaic conjunction 'an' means the same as 'if'. It comes in one of Mother Goose's Nursery Rhymes:

> If 'ifs' and 'ans'
> Were pots and pans
> There'd be no work for tinkers!

Tinkers are menders of pots and pans, and if 'if' were magically transformed into a new kitchen utensil every time it was said, there would be no need for their services. But there is always 'if'.

A similar proverb is IF WISHES WERE HORSES, BEGGARS WOULD RIDE (330).

323 If it were not for hope, the heart would break

When things are very difficult, what prevents us from giving up in despair is the hope that things will get better.

324 If one sheep leaps over the ditch, all the rest will follow

It is in the nature of sheep to follow each other, yet there must be one sheep braver than the rest, one that has to set an example before they will take the risk. We find in Scott's *Old Mortality*: 'One sheep will leap the ditch when another goes first.'

Does not the same apply to us human beings?

Of course there is the other side to it: the leading sheep may be a 'reluctant hero' pushed from behind.

325 If the blind lead the blind, both shall fall into the ditch

This is from Matthew, xv, 14. It means that those without knowledge themselves should not try to teach the ignorant.

'He claimed to know a good deal about television sets, which was more than I did. He asked me for a screwdriver, tinkered about for half an hour, then said, "Right. Now you can switch on." I did. There was a blue flash and the set caught alight. Talk about the blind leading the blind! The fellow hadn't a clue.'

326 If the cap fits, wear it

If you think I am talking about *you*, you are welcome to that opinion.

'I don't like people who tell lies,' said Peter.

'Meaning me?' demanded Paul.

Peter shrugged his shoulders and replied: 'If the cap fits, wear it.'

**327 If the mountain will not come to Mahomet, Mahomet must go
to the mountain**

If you are unable to get your own way, you must bow to the
inevitable.

'I know I refused to do it, but somebody's got to, so if no one
else will take it on, I suppose I shall have to do it myself. It's the
old, old story of Mahomet and the mountain.'

This proverb has not the same meaning as the story from which
it is drawn. Mahomet did not bow to the inevitable; he snatched
victory from defeat. The story runs that the Arabs were reluctant
to accept his teaching until he had performed a miracle. He
ordered Mount Safa, outside the holy city of Mecca, to come to
him. When it did not move he said:

'God is merciful. Had it obeyed me it would have fallen on us
and destroyed us. I will therefore go to the mountain and thank
God that He has had mercy on us.'

328 If there were no clouds, we should not enjoy the sun

We can have too much of a good thing; and happier times seem
all the happier if they are interrupted now and again by gloomy
spells. This is sometimes basely used as an excuse for accepting
poverty, overwork and other hardships.

329 If two men ride on a horse, one must ride behind

There cannot be two leaders in any enterprise.

The man riding behind must leave it to the man in front to
guide the horse. Similarly, on a tandem the man in front steers
the machine and applies the brakes.

Other proverbs on the theme of leadership are DON'T SPEAK TO
THE MAN AT THE WHEEL (145); HE THAT CANNOT OBEY CANNOT
COMMAND (271); IT NEEDS MORE SKILL THAN I CAN TELL TO
PLAY THE SECOND FIDDLE WELL (371); THROUGH OBEDIENCE
LEARN TO COMMAND (683).

330 If wishes were horses, beggars would ride

This means the same as IF 'IFS' AND 'ANS' WERE POTS AND
PANS . . . (322).

331 If you cannot bite never show your teeth

To show your teeth is, figuratively, to leave it in no doubt that you are ready to attack or to defend yourself. Should you be in no position to take such active steps, you should not threaten that you will do so. DISCRETION IS THE BETTER PART OF VALOUR (117).

332 If you do not like it you may lump it
The verb 'to lump' means 'to put up with ungraciously'. This is the answer to anyone who complains about something that is unavoidable.

'We've missed the last bus, so we'll have to walk home.'

'You don't expect me to tramp three miles in the rain, do you?'

'There's no help for it. It's the only way of getting home, and if you don't like it you can lump it.'

333 If you run after two hares you will catch neither
Don't try to do two things at once. Concentrate on one or the other.

A similar proverb is BETWEEN TWO STOOLS YOU FALL TO THE GROUND (51).

334 If you sing before breakfast, you will cry before night
If you start the day in too joyful a mood, the good spirits are unlikely to last the day out. This is the warning of the pessimist.

335 If you want a thing well done, do it yourself
This is good advice up to a point, yet an employer who does not delegate authority because he does not trust his staff to carry out his instructions is not only increasing his own burdens but also depriving his staff of all initiative.

After all, WHY KEEP A DOG AND BARK YOURSELF? (764).

336 If you want peace, prepare for war
By arming itself to meet aggression, a country reduces the risk of being attacked.

George Washington said in his address to Congress on 8th January, 1790:

'To be prepared for war is the most effectual means of preserving peace.'

337 Ill news comes apace
This is the old version of BAD NEWS TRAVELS FAST (27).

338 An ill payer never wants an excuse

Here 'wants' means 'lacks'. A man who keeps his creditors waiting always has an excuse ready for not paying their bills.

339 Ill weeds grow apace

Though the plants we value will not grow in our gardens without endless care and attention, worthless weeds always thrive; and worthless people seem to thrive also.

340 Imitation is the sincerest form of flattery

To flatter is to give too much praise, to compliment unduly. By its very nature it is insincere, not an expression of honest opinion. If, however, we imitate a person – that is, do as he does – we are paying him a sincere compliment.

'My neighbour on the left thinks I made a magnificent job of returfing our front lawn; he can't speak too highly of it.'

'What about the chap on the other side? Is he full of praise too?'

'No; but as soon as he saw how mine turned out, he began to returf his own.'

'They say that imitation is the sincerest form of flattery!'

341 In a calm sea every man is a pilot

We are all ready to do the other fellow's job – or offer advice – when there is no risk attached, but we are not so eager to volunteer when danger threatens.

D'Arcy Wentworth Thompson, the English scholar, put this into verse:

> When winds are steady and skies are clear,
> Every hand the ship must steer;
> But soon as ever the wild winds blow,
> Every hand would go below.

342 In for a penny, in for a pound

Once we have committed ourselves to some extent in an undertaking, we may as well go through with it.

A similar proverb is AS WELL BE HANGED FOR A SHEEP AS A LAMB (22).

343 In peace prepare for war

Another version of IF YOU WANT PEACE, PREPARE FOR WAR (336).

344 In the country of the blind, the one-eyed man is king
If a man shows greater ability than those around him he has a decided advantage, even though his talents are not really outstanding. Metaphorically, even with only one eye he rules like a king over his sightless subjects.

345 In vino veritas
The original version of IN WINE THERE IS TRUTH (346).

346 In wine there is truth
A sober man keeps a guard on his tongue, holding back anything he wishes to hide. Strong drink unseals his lips and he tells everything. Hence a man is more likely to speak the truth when he is drunk than when he is sober.

The Latin tag, *In vino veritas*, is more often used than the English version.

A similar proverb is WHAT SOBERNESS CONCEALS, DRUNKENNESS REVEALS (738).

347 It is a foolish bird that soils its own nest
Just as a bird doesn't dirty its own nest, so human beings shouldn't do anything to harm what is close to them. In other words, don't commit your indiscretions too near home!

348 It is a foolish sheep that makes the wolf his confessor
Never confide in anyone unless you are sure that he will respect your confidence and will not turn to his own advantage what you have said to him.

'I just happened to mention to this chap in the pub that I'd forgotten to lock up the silver before I came out, and when I got back home later in the evening, the house had been broken into and all the silver was gone.'

'That's your own silly fault. Never give secrets away to strangers in pubs. It's a foolish sheep that makes the wolf his confessor.'

A similar proverb is NEVER TELL YOUR ENEMY THAT YOUR FOOT ACHES (495).

349 It's a long lane that has no turning
Bad times don't go on for ever. Sooner or later things will improve.

Similar proverbs are THE DARKEST HOUR IS THAT BEFORE THE DAWN (103); THE LONGEST DAY MUST HAVE AN END (424).

350   It is a sad heart that never rejoices

Sometimes 'poor' is used instead of 'sad'. Even the most con-
firmed of pessimists can't be miserable all the time. We can't look
for ever on the gloomy side of things.

Mrs Stevens looked up from the letter she had been reading at
the breakfast table.

'It's from Mother,' she said to her husband. 'She can't come
and stay with us after all.'

'It's a sad heart,' said Mr Stevens from behind his paper, 'that
never rejoices.'

351   It is a sad house where the hen crows louder than the cock

No home is happy in which the husband is such a weakling that it
is his wife who gives all the orders.

352   It's an ill wind that blows nobody any good

When all ocean-going ships depended upon the wind to blow
them along, a wind favourable to a vessel travelling east was
unfavourable to one travelling west; but as ships were voyaging
all over the globe – one eastward, one westward, another to north
or south – there was seldom a wind 'blew nobody any good', that
did not benefit anyone at all.

By extension this proverb means that every calamity, loss or
misfortune is of advantage to somebody. If Mr Harrison's house
is struck by lightning, Mr Johnson makes money out of repairing
it; and if Mr Wilkins misses the last train home, the taxi-driver
profits in consequence.

353   It is as well to know which way the wind blows

It is as well to know what developments are likely, or what is the
state of public opinion. 'To know which way the cat is going to
jump' has much the same meaning.

'I'm going to make some inquiries,' said the politician. 'As soon
as I know which way the wind blows, I'll decide which line I'm
going to take. I'm not going to be on the losing side if I can help it.'

354   It is better to give than to take

The source of this is Acts, xx, 35:

'I have shewed you all things, how that so labouring we ought
to support the weak, and to remember the words of the Lord
Jesus, how he said, It is more blessed to give than to receive.'

355 It is better to wear out than to rust out

It is better to die as the result of being worn out with activity than as the result of doing nothing. The proverb is often quoted by elderly people who remain active in old age and seem to do more than old people should do.

356 It's dogged that does it

Here 'dogged' (two syllables with the stress on the first) means 'persistent'. The proverb teaches perseverance and the determination to succeed. Stick to it and you will achieve your object.

Other proverbs on this theme are CONSTANT DRIPPING WEARS AWAY THE STONE (90); IF AT FIRST YOU DON'T SUCCEED, TRY, TRY, TRY AGAIN (320); LITTLE BY LITTLE AND BIT BY BIT (415); LITTLE STROKES FELL GREAT OAKS (419); ROME WAS NOT BUILT IN A DAY (588); SLOW BUT SURE WINS THE RACE (603); WHERE THERE'S A WILL THERE'S A WAY (755).

357 It is easier to pull down than to build

It is easier to destroy than to create. It is easier to criticize than to make constructive suggestions.

358 It is easy to be wise after the event

When something has ended badly, it is easy to say what should have been done to ensure success. Foresight is being wise before the event; being wise after the event is called 'hindsight'. Many people are gifted with hindsight!

'If I'd been captain I should have put young Lawson on to bowl much earlier and then we should have won.'

'Bonnie Prince Charlie got as far as Derby and then retreated. If he hadn't been persuaded not to march on to London he'd have become King of England. What a lost opportunity!'

'You went wrong when you . . .'

'Why on earth he didn't . . .'

'It sticks out a mile that instead of . . .'

359 It is easy to bear the misfortunes of others

It is easy for us to tell others to be cheerful in the face of misfortune, because we don't have to suffer the hardship ourselves. It perhaps suggests too that we all secretly find satisfaction in other people's misfortunes because we feel pleased to have avoided them ourselves.

360   It is good fishing in troubled waters

Trout and other fish are more easily caught when the surface of the water is disturbed. Figuratively, 'to fish in troubled waters' is to take advantage of other people's difficulties, particularly in times of general unrest or national emergency. Those who made large profits out of illegally selling rationed goods during World War II were fishing in troubled waters. So is the scoundrel who picks the pockets of a man lying unconscious on the road after being knocked down by a passing car.

361   It is ill jesting with edged tools

It is dangerous to play with sharp tools. Similarly it is dangerous to meddle with anything that may get you into trouble. For example, to take 'pep' pills condemned by the medical profession is to jest with edged tools.

362   It is ill striving against the stream

It is easier to adapt ourselves to circumstances than to fight against them.

363   It is ill waiting for dead men's shoes

To wait for dead men's shoes is to wait for the death of a person with the expectancy of succeeding to his possessions or office. This sometimes takes a long time, so the waiting is 'ill' – that is, hard to endure.

'Ability counts for nothing in this firm,' complained young Clarke. 'All you can do is wait for dead men's shoes.'

364   It is love that makes the world go round

Love brings children into the world and so keeps human life from becoming extinct.

365   It is never too late to mend

Here 'to mend' means 'to reform, to mend one's ways'. It is never too late to turn over a new leaf and lead a better life.

366   It is no use crying over spilt milk

It was a great pity that it happened, but there's nothing we can do about it now. Don't bewail the past. WHAT'S DONE CANNOT BE UNDONE (729).

367 It is no use spoiling the ship for a ha'p'orth of tar
This teaches the folly of false economy; of failing to achieve one's purpose by trying to save in a small detail; of marring an effect in order to avoid spending a trifling extra amount. A man who buys an expensive new overcoat and continues to wear his shabby old hat with it is spoiling the ship for a ha'p'orth of tar.

The Shorter Oxford Dictionary reminds us that 'spoiling the ship' should be 'losing the sheep'. '*Sheep* is dialectally pronounced *ship* in many parts of England, and the tar was used to protect sore places on sheep from the attacks of flies.'

Similar proverbs are A STITCH IN TIME SAVES NINE (619); WHO REPAIRS NOT HIS GUTTERS REPAIRS HIS WHOLE HOUSE (763).

368 It is the unexpected that always happens
Another version of this is NOTHING IS SO CERTAIN AS THE UNEXPECTED (518). A similar French proverb is: 'Nothing is certain but uncertainty.' The state of things as they are cannot be relied upon to continue. Something unforeseen is liable to happen at any moment.

369 It is too late to lock the stable when the horse has been stolen
It is useless to take precautions after something has happened that could have been foreseen and guarded against. The French version is, 'After the death, the doctor.'

When his father gave Tommy an air-gun as a birthday present, Miss Watson, who lived next door, suggested that a small boy should not have so dangerous a toy. After Tommy had shot Miss Watson's cat, his father took the air-gun away from him. We do not know what Miss Watson said about this, but a very suitable remark would have been, 'It is too late to lock the stable door when the horse has been stolen.'

370 It is useless to flog a dead horse
It is a waste of time to try to revive interest in a worn-out or forgotten subject, or to argue about something that was settled long since.

'I said it at the time and I say it again that when they built the new bypass they should have taken it round the north of the town, not round the south.'

'Why bring that up again? Nothing can be done about it now. You're flogging a dead horse.'
See also HARP NOT FOR EVER ON THE SAME STRING (263).

371 It needs more skill than I can tell to play the second fiddle well
This couplet was composed by Charles H. Spurgeon, the famous Baptist minister and orator.

The leading performer in an orchestra is the first violin. By extension, to play first violin is to take the leading part in any enterprise. A familiar or contemptuous name for a violin is a fiddle, so to play second fiddle is to take a subordinate part. To play the second fiddle well is to give loyal support to your immediate superior.

Similar proverbs are HE THAT CANNOT OBEY CANNOT COMMAND (271); IF TWO MEN RIDE ON A HORSE, ONE MUST RIDE BEHIND (329); THROUGH OBEDIENCE LEARN TO COMMAND (683)

372 It never rains but it pours
In modern English this would read, 'It never rains without pouring.' The meaning is that events, especially misfortunes, always come together.

'What a day it's been,' sighed Mrs Wood. 'First I burnt out the kettle, then the electricity fused, then Mrs Mopp didn't arrive, then the butcher didn't deliver the meat in time for lunch, then the doctor called and said Tommy's got measles. It was one thing after another. They say it never rains but it pours.'
See also MISFORTUNES NEVER COME SINGLY (463).

373 It takes all sorts to make a world
We are not all alike. We differ from each other in many ways – physically, mentally and morally. Some of us are good sorts, some of us are bad sorts, and some of us are a bit of each. So we must be charitable and allow everyone the right to exist. LIVE AND LET LIVE (422).

374 It takes two to make a quarrel
A quarrel is an angry dispute between two persons. Tom cannot quarrel with himself; nor can he quarrel with Dick if Dick does not wish to quarrel with *him*. Tom may lose his temper, but as long as Dick does not lose his, there can be no quarrel. The pro-

verb is often used like this:

'I'll admit we both lost our tempers, but it wasn't my fault. He started it.'

'It takes two to make a quarrel.'

See also A SOFT ANSWER TURNETH AWAY WRATH (605).

375 It will be all the same a hundred years hence
In a hundred years' time we shall all be dead, so why should we worry about our present troubles and cares? This may contain a sound warning against worrying too much about the present, but, taken too far, as it often is, it produces the cynical attitude of 'Why bother at all about anything? Who cares?'

J

376 A Jack of all trades is master of none
Here 'Jack' is a nickname for a general labourer, one who does odd jobs and can turn his hand to anything. A 'trade' in this sense is an occupation – the trade of a carpenter, the trade of a brick-layer, the trade of a plumber, a mechanic, a blacksmith. Jack may have had some experience in these and other trades, yet is still master of none – that is, not a really skilled workman in any trade. The proverb therefore suggests that if you want to get on in the world you should concentrate on one thing and learn to do it well.

377 Jam tomorrow and jam yesterday – but never jam today
If there is one day of the week that we enjoy more than the other six, today never seems to be that day.

The proverb is a quotation from *Through the Looking-Glass* by Lewis Carroll. The White Queen wants Alice to be her lady's-maid and offers her twopence a week and jam every other day.

Alice couldn't help laughing, as she said 'I don't want you to hire *me* – and I don't care for jam.'

'It's very good jam,' said the Queen.

'Well, I don't want any *today*, at any rate.'

'You couldn't have it if you *did* want it,' the Queen said. 'The rule is, jam tomorrow and jam yesterdav – but never jam *today*.'

'It *must* come sometimes to "jam today", ' Alice objected.

'No, it can't,' said the Queen. 'It's jam every other day: today isn't any *cther* day, you know.'

A similar proverb is THE GOLDEN AGE WAS NEVER THE PRESENT AGE (244).

378   Judge not, that ye be not judged
Think before you criticize others, for you may be criticized yourself in return.

The source is Matthew, vii, 1. It is part of the sermon on the mount and reads in the Moffatt translation: 'Judge not, that you may not be judged yourselves; for as you judge so you will be judged, and the measures you deal out to others will be dealt out to yourselves.'

Similar proverbs are: DO AS YOU WOULD BE DONE BY (121); THOSE WHO LIVE IN GLASS HOUSES SHOULD NOT THROW STONES (680).

K

379   Keep something for a rainy day
Here 'rainy day' means 'time of trouble or misfortune'. The advice given is: 'You may be earning good money now, but don't spend it all. Put something aside every week to meet possible emergencies in the future.'

A similar proverb is WASTE NOT, WANT NOT (715).

380   Kill not the goose that lays the golden eggs
A Greek fable tells of a man who possessed a goose that laid golden eggs. Impatient and avaricious by nature, he was not satisfied with one golden egg every day or so, but wanted all the eggs at once. So he killed the goose, opened her up and – well, you can guess the rest of the story.

When we use this proverb we mean that anyone who claims more than he is already receiving is very likely to get nothing at all in future.

Young Alan had a very generous uncle who gave him five shillings every time he came to tea. Alan wanted a bicycle, so the next time his uncle called he asked him for ten pounds instead of five shillings.

'Ten pounds?' exclaimed his uncle.

'Well, you can afford it, can't you?' demanded Alan rudely.

This annoyed his uncle so much that Alan did not get his bicycle – or any more five-shilling tips. He had killed the goose that laid the golden eggs.

381 Kind hearts are more than coronets
It is the character of a man that counts, not the nobility of his descent.

The proverb is a quotation from *Lady Clara Vere de Vere*, a poem by Tennyson:

> From yon blue heavens above us bent,
>   The gardener Adam and his wife
> Smile at the claims of long descent.
>   Howe'er it be, it seems to me
> 'Tis only noble to be good.
>   Kind hearts are more than coronets,
> And simple faith than Norman blood.

382 Know your own faults before blaming others for theirs
This means the same as JUDGE NOT, THAT YE BE NOT JUDGED (378). A similar proverb is THOSE WHO LIVE IN GLASS HOUSES SHOULD NOT THROW STONES (680).

383 Knowledge is power
The greater our knowledge, the greater our influence on others.

L

384 The labourer is worthy of his hire
Anyone who works for someone else deserves to be paid for it, if not in cash, then in kind. The source is Luke, x, 7. Jesus sent seventy disciples in pairs to every town and place that he intended to visit himself. He told them before they went that they were to spread the news of the reign of God and heal the sick. 'And into whatsoever house ye enter, first say Peace be to this house. And if the son of peace be there, your peace shall rest upon it . . . And in the same house remain, eating and drinking such things as they give; for the labourer is worthy of his hire.' In this context a labourer was one who worked in the service of God.

385 The last drop makes the cup run over
This has the same meaning as THE LAST STRAW BREAKS THE CAMEL'S BACK (386).

386 The last straw breaks the camel's back
If you increase a camel's burden straw by straw, eventually you will load him with one straw too many and his back will be broken. The phrase 'the last straw' refers to something that, although small in itself, comes after many other troublesome things and produces at last the feeling of being intolerable.

Mr Jackson's neighbours had very noisy children. He put up with it as long as he could, but the last straw was when the boy next door decided to learn to play the bugle.

387 Laugh and grow fat
This is merely encouragement to be cheerful rather than solemn. Lean people tend to be more solemn than fat ones. So laugh and grow fat like the cheerful ones.

388 Laugh and the world laughs with you, weep and you weep alone
If you are in a cheerful mood it is easier to get people to share your interests and feelings than if you are solemn or sad, when people tend to keep away from you.

Though the general idea of the proverb was current long before that, it was given its present form in 1883 by Ella Wheeler Wilcox. It comes in her poem called *Solitude*:

> Laugh and the world laughs with you,
>   Weep and you weep alone,
> For the sad old earth must borrow its mirth,
>   But has trouble enough of its own.

389 Learn to walk before you run
Knowledge cannot be acquired all at once; it must be gained step by step. Don't try to spell 'catastrophe' if you cannot spell 'cat'!

390 Least said, soonest mended
Here 'mended' has the sense of making amends or atoning for some misdeed. The proverb means that long explanations and apologies are of little use and tend to make matters worse.

See also LET BYGONES BE BYGONES (393).

391   Lend your money and lose your friend
A similar proverb is WHEN I LENT I HAD A FRIEND; WHEN I ASKED
HE WAS UNKIND (745). If your friend finds himself unable to
repay the debt, he will avoid you and may well say bad things
about you to justify his conduct. There is a Portuguese proverb
that says: 'If you would make an enemy, lend a man money, and
ask it of him again.'
   See also NEITHER A BORROWER NOR A LENDER BE (483).

392   The leopard cannot change his spots
The accepted figurative meaning of this is that men cannot change
their characters, and just as a leopard is born spotted and will
always be so, a man with a wicked nature is born wicked and will
never be anything else. The more exact meaning is that, although
not basically wicked, a man can become in the course of time so
degraded and sunk in ungodliness that there is no more chance of
changing his ways than there is of a leopard's changing his spots.
   The source is Jeremiah, xiii, 23: 'Can the Ethiopian change his
skin, or the leopard his spots?'

393   Let bygones be bygones
Bygones are things that happened in the past. To let bygones be
bygones is to forgive and forget.
   'I'm sorry I lost my temper and said things I didn't really mean,'
said Colin.
   'Then I suggest we let bygones be bygones and start afresh,'
said Stephen, extending his hand.
   A similar proverb is LEAST SAID, SOONEST MENDED (390).

394   Let not the sun go down on your wrath
If you are angry with anybody, don't let your bitter feelings last
overnight. The source is Ephesians, iv, 26.

395   Let not thy left hand know what thy right hand doeth
Keep secret any help you give to the poor; don't boast of your alms-
giving. The source is Matthew, vi, 1–4.

396   Let not your wits go wool-gathering
Don't allow your mind to wander. Think what you are doing.

Literally, to go wool-gathering is to go hither and thither collecting fragments of wool torn from sheep by bushes and the like.

397 Let sleeping dogs lie

Don't do anything that will stir up unnecessary trouble.

'The woman next door always has clothes hanging out on the line. It looks awful. I've half a mind to write a sharp note to her husband. What do you think?'

'Might make matters worse. I'd let sleeping dogs lie if I were you.'

A similar proverb is WAKE NOT A SLEEPING LION (712).

398 Let the buyer beware

Before he parts with his cash a purchaser should satisfy himself that whatever he is buying is in good condition and worth the money he is paying for it. It is too late to complain after the transaction has been completed. The Latin version is *Caveat emptor* (77).

399 Let the cobbler stick to his last

A cobbler is one who makes his living by repairing boots and shoes. The term is also used for that superior craftsman, a shoemaker, who uses a wooden or metal model called a 'last' for shaping the footwear he produces. But however clever he may be at his trade, he should not try to give advice on other matters.

The Roman writer, Pliny the Elder, tells this story about the painter Apelles: 'He was in the habit of hanging his pictures where they could be seen by the passers-by, and listening to their comments. One day a shoemaker criticized the shoes in a certain picture, and found next day that they had been repainted. Proud of his success as a critic, he began to find fault with the thigh of the picture, when Apelles called out from behind the canvas, "Shoemaker, don't go above your last!" ' (*Stevenson's Book of Quotations.*)

The proverb applies to anyone who tries to teach someone else his business. A plumber does not welcome the advice of an electrician; and an electrician does not welcome the advice of a plumber.

400 Let the world wag
Let it wag, let it slide, let it go, let it slip, let it sink, let it pass. The last word varies, but the meaning is always the same: 'Let the world do what it likes. I regard the course of events with complete unconcern. It matters nothing to me what it does as long as it leaves me alone.' A sixteenth-century philosopher decided to 'let the world wag and take mine ease in mine inn'.

401 A liar is not believed when he tells the truth
He is like the mischievous young shepherd who roused the village a number of times by crying 'Wolf!' when there was no wolf. The time arrived when a wolf did attack the flock, but nobody took any notice of his warning shouts of 'Wolf! Wolf!'

402 Liars should have good memories
If we always tell the truth we are unlikely to contradict ourselves; but if we resort to lies we are liable, when asked a question for a second time, to forget what our answer was on the first occasion.
'I tell you I couldn't have done the murder,' protested the man suspected of the crime, 'because I was up in London when it happened.'
'Which part of London?'
'Battersea.'
'Last time we asked you you said it was Bermondsey. Come on, let's have the truth for a change.'
See also ONE LIE MAKES MANY (533).

403 Life is not all beer and skittles
Life is not all fun and games. We have our pleasant times, but we have our serious ones too. As Trilby says in the book by George Du Maurier that bears her name: 'Well, I've got to go back to work. Life ain't all beer and skittles, and more's the pity; but what's the odds, so long as you're happy?'

404 Life is short and time is swift
Enjoy life while you can, for you will not live for ever. GATHER YE ROSEBUDS WHILE YE MAY (229).
Other proverbs on the theme of taking advantage of one's opportunities are listed under OPPORTUNITY SELDOM KNOCKS TWICE (546).

405   Life is sweet
This is to be found in *Lavengro* by George Borrow:

'Life is sweet, brother.'
'Do you think so?'
'Think so! – There's night and day, brother, both sweet things; sun, moon, and stars, brother, all sweet things; there's likewise a wind on the heath. Life is very sweet, brother; who would wish to die?'

It is not, of course, the origin of the proverb, which dates right back to the fourteenth century.

406   Light not a candle to the sun
Don't try to throw more light on a matter that is already quite clear enough. Don't try to explain the obvious. Don't take the easy course of repeating what is already known, instead of making original researches into what is not known.

407   A light purse makes a heavy heart
We cannot be cheerful when we have money troubles. The reverse, of course, is A HEAVY PURSE MAKES A LIGHT HEART (300).

408   Lightly come, lightly go
This means the same as EASY COME, EASY GO (160).

409   Like father, like son
Many sons take after their fathers, not only in looks but also in character. Some sons are described as 'a chip of the old block' – a small piece of the same wood as a large piece. Sometimes the inherited characteristics are not good ones.

'Mrs Davis had enough trouble with her husband until he deserted her. The sad thing is that the eldest boy already drinks like a fish.'
'Like father, like son, eh?'
See also WHAT IS BRED IN THE BONE WILL NEVER COME OUT OF THE FLESH (728).

410   Like master, like man
Here 'man' means 'servant' or 'workman'. If the master is a good employer, the man is a good employee – and vice versa. 'Like mistress, like maid' also applies.

411 Like will to like
We all tend to seek the company of those whose tastes or interests are similar to our own. This proverb has the same meaning as BIRDS OF A FEATHER FLOCK TOGETHER (54) and MEN ARE KNOWN BY THE COMPANY THEY KEEP (455). Proverbs dealing with the dangers of keeping bad company are listed under the first of these (54).

412 A lion may come to be beholden to a mouse
There are times when the weak can help the strong. A rich or eminent man should treat a poor or obscure man with consideration, for one day he may be beholden to him – that is, indebted to him – for doing him a great service.

It is the story of the lion in the fable who spared the life of a mouse and was later rewarded by the mouse, who gnawed through the net in which the lion had been trapped.

413 Listeners hear no good of themselves
This means the same as EAVESDROPPERS NEVER HEAR ANY GOOD OF THEMSELVES (161).

414 Little and often fills the purse
Small sums of money frequently received soon mount up. MANY A LITTLE MAKES A MICKLE (446).

415 Little by little and bit by bit
This proverb teaches patience and perseverance. Don't be discouraged by the size of the task you have to do. Stick to it and you will achieve success.

Other proverbs on this theme are CONSTANT DRIPPING WEARS AWAY THE STONE (90); IF AT FIRST YOU DON'T SUCCEED, TRY, TRY, TRY AGAIN (320); IT'S DOGGED THAT DOES IT (356); LITTLE STROKES FELL GREAT OAKS (419); ROME WAS NOT BUILT IN A DAY (588); SLOW BUT SURE WINS THE RACE (603); WHERE THERE'S A WILL THERE'S A WAY (755).

416 A little help is worth a deal of pity
This is similar to ACTIONS SPEAK LOUDER THAN WORDS (3). It is better to help persons who are in trouble than to say how sorry you are for them. For example, when Mrs Pemberton's kitchen was flooded out by a heavy storm of rain, Mrs Trulove, who lived

next door, was very sympathetic indeed. She was still telling Mrs Pemberton how grieved she was that such a thing should have happened to her neighbour, when Mrs Young came across from over the road with a bucket and mop to help Mrs Pemberton to clear up the mess.

417   A little learning is a dangerous thing
People with a little knowledge are often unaware of their ignorance and are consequently easily misled.

The quotation is from Pope's *Essay on Criticism* (1711).

A similar proverb is THERE IS NO ROYAL ROAD TO LEARNING (664).

418   Little pitchers have long ears
Sometimes 'wide' is used instead of 'long'. A pitcher is an earthenware jug with two ears instead of a handle. They are called 'ears' because they resemble human ears in the way they project from the pitcher. 'Little pitchers have long ears' is another way of saying 'Not in front of the children'. Although they may not give that impression young children often take in every word spoken by their elders.

'You know who I am, don't you?' the visitor asked Tommy.

'Oh, yes,' replied Tommy. 'Dad says you're the biggest idiot he's ever met.'

419   Little strokes fell great oaks
This proverb teaches patience and perseverance. Given enough time and the determination to succeed, one could cut down even the largest of trees with a penknife.

Other proverbs on this theme are CONSTANT DRIPPING WEARS AWAY THE STONE (90); IF AT FIRST YOU DON'T SUCCEED, TRY, TRY, TRY AGAIN (320); IT'S DOGGED THAT DOES IT (356); LITTLE BY LITTLE AND BIT BY BIT (415); ROME WAS NOT BUILT IN A DAY (588); SLOW BUT SURE WINS THE RACE (603); WHERE THERE'S A WILL THERE'S A WAY (755).

420   Little things please little minds
People of limited intelligence are interested only in unimportant things. As Ovid wrote: 'Frivolous minds are won by trifles.'

421   Live and learn
Experience is a good teacher. The longer we live, the more we learn.

The saying is often used in a half-humorous way, as if with a shrug of the shoulders.

'I bought some walnuts from a barrow-boy in East Street, and when I got them home and cracked them open, nearly all of them were bad.'

'Ah, well. We live and learn.'

422 Live and let live

Other people have as much right to live as we have, and all of us have failings, so to remain on friendly terms with our neighbours we should overlook their shortcomings in the hope that they will overlook ours.

A similar proverb is IT TAKES ALL SORTS TO MAKE A WORLD (373).

423 Live not to eat, but eat to live

This rather puritanical proverb warns us that eating should not be the main purpose of life. We should, on the contrary, eat just enough to lead a useful life.

424 The longest day must have an end

However long and wearisome the day may seem, it must inevitably be followed by night and come to an end. In the same way, all tedious tasks are finished at last.

A similar proverb is IT'S A LONG LANE THAT HAS NO TURNING (349).

425 The longest way round is the nearest way home

Short cuts can involve one in difficulties. It is better to follow the correct procedure in anything than to try to save time by scamping the work. For example, it may seem quicker to redecorate the sitting-room by putting the new paint straight on to the old, whereas the correct way – and in the end the quickest – is to prepare the work thoroughly before applying the new paint.

See also THE BEATEN ROAD IS THE SAFEST (34).

426 Look before you leap

Never act hastily. Consider carefully what you are going to do before you do it. It might be said that this contradicts the other proverb, HE WHO HESITATES IS LOST (291), but this is not necessarily so; if you look before you leap, decide that you can get across in safety, then hesitate at the very last moment, you'll probably fall in!

427　Lookers-on see most of the game

Those watching the game get a better impression of what is going on than those taking part in it. They have a wider view than have the individual players, and more often than not have no hesitation in telling them where they have gone wrong! Usually this applies to outdoor games such as football, but by extension 'game' means anything in which human beings are involved.

'Doesn't he know that his wife's being unfaithful to him, and doesn't *she* know he's being unfaithful to *her*? If they don't, everybody else does!'

'Lookers-on see most of the game.'

428　Love is blind

Those in love are blind to each other's faults.

429　Love laughs at locksmiths

This means much the same as LOVE WILL FIND A WAY (433). The source is *Venus and Adonis*, the long poem by Shakespeare:

> Were beauty under twenty locks kept fast,
> Yet love breaks through, and picks them all at last.

430　Love me little, love me long

Do not let your passion for a person become too strong, for it may soon burn itself out. Mild affection is more likely to be long-lived. In Shakespeare's *Romeo and Juliet*, Father Laurence advises Romeo:

> These violent delights have violent ends,
> And in their triumph die; like fire and powder
> Which as they kiss consume: the sweetest honey
> Is loathsome in his own deliciousness,
> And in the taste confounds the appetite:
> Therefore love moderately; long love doth so
> Too swift arrives as tardy as too slow.

431　Love me, love my dog

Dr Brewer wrote of this: 'If you love me you must put up with my faults, my little ways, or (sometimes) my friends. A rather selfish maxim!'

432   The love of money is the root of all evil
All kinds of wickedness and tribulation spring from the desire to become rich.

The source is I Timothy, vi, 10. Here it is in its context:

7   For we brought nothing into this world, and it is certain that we can carry nothing out.
8   And having food and raiment let us be therewith content.
9   But they that will be rich fall into temptation and a snare, and into many foolish and hurtful lusts, which drown men in destruction and perdition.
10   For the love of money is the root of all evil: which while some coveted after, they have erred from the faith, and pierced themselves through with many sorrows.

Note that it is the love of money that is the root of all evil, not money itself. 'Money is the root of all evil' is a misquotation.

433   Love will find a way
Love has such power that it will overcome all difficulties.

434   Love your neighbour, yet pull not down your fence
This means the same as A HEDGE BETWEEN KEEPS FRIENDSHIP GREEN (301).

M

435   Make haste slowly
Don't do anything in too much of a hurry. MORE HASTE, LESS SPEED (470).

436   Make hay while the sun shines
Do not wait until tomorrow, for rain may ruin the harvest. By extension this means that we should always take advantage of favourable circumstances.

'Why are you writing science fiction,' asked the friend of an author, 'instead of the historical novels you used to write?'

'Because,' replied the author, 'science fiction has become very popular and I'm making hay while the sun shines.'

A similar proverb is STRIKE WHILE THE IRON IS HOT (624). Other proverbs on the theme of opportunity are listed under OPPORTUNITY SELDOM KNOCKS TWICE (546).

437   Make the best of a bad bargain
Here 'bargain' does not refer to something bought cheaply, but to an agreement made between two parties. When one party realizes too late that the agreement is more to the other party's advantage than his own, he is said to have made a bad bargain; but as the agreement is binding on both parties, he has no alternative but to make the best of it, to accept the fact that he has lost on the deal.

In a figurative sense, to make the best of a bad bargain is to try to be cheerful in the face of an unhappy situation and do your best with it, as in the next proverb.

438   Make the best of a bad job
This teaches the same philosophy as the one above. Here 'job' does not refer to working, but to a state of affairs. To make the best of a bad job is to accept one's present position with equanimity, to put up with an unfavourable or uncomfortable state of affairs.

'We ran out of petrol when we were miles from anywhere, and as it was gone midnight we had to make the best of a bad job and sleep in the car.'

439   Make yourself all honey and the flies will devour you
If you are too obsequious, too servile, others will treat you with contempt. Don't be a yes-man.

Similar proverbs are DON'T CRY STINKING FISH (127); DON'T MAKE YOURSELF A MOUSE, OR THE CAT WILL EAT YOU (136).

440   A man can only die once
The fact of dying can only be experienced once. This is meant to console us with the thought that if death comes now it won't have to be experienced later.

441   A man is as old as he feels, and a woman as old as she looks
As long as a man feels well and strong it does not matter how old

he looks. With a woman, however, looks are more important, since a woman tends to be judged by them; if she looks old, people will think of her as old and therefore 'past it'.

442 A man of words and not of deeds is like a garden full of weeds
If a man does nothing but talk, he produces nothing of value. Similar proverbs are ACTIONS SPEAK LOUDER THAN WORDS (3); THE GREATEST TALKERS ARE THE LEAST DOERS (256).

443 Man proposes, God disposes
Man expresses his intention of doing a thing, but it is God who decides whether it is to be done. This is really an expression of fatalism, as God here represents Fate, against which it is useless to struggle. Hence the expression *Deo volente*, abbreviated D.V., which means 'God willing'.
'I shall see you again next year, D.V.'

444 A man without a smiling face must not open a shop
This comes to us from the Chinese. A shopkeeper who behaves in a surly way is unlikely to attract customers.

445 Manners maketh man
Another version is 'Manners make the man'. A person is often judged by his manners rather than his character, especially on first acquaintance, so in this sense manners are all-important.

446 Many a little makes a mickle
This advises thrift. If you start with a little and continually add a little, you will eventually have a mickle, which is an Anglo-Saxon word meaning 'much'. If, for example, you put aside fifty pence a week you will have £130 in five years.
The Scottish version, 'Many a mickle makes a muckle', uses 'mickle' instead of 'little', and muckle' instead of 'mickle', but it means the same thing as the above.
Similar proverbs are EVERY LITTLE HELPS (179); TAKE CARE OF THE PENCE AND THE POUNDS WILL TAKE CARE OF THEMSELVES (631).

447 Many hands make light work
The more people there are to carry out a task, the less each has to do, and the more quickly is the work finished.

It has been said that this proverb is contradicted by TOO MANY
COOKS SPOIL THE BROTH (695), but, to quote another saying,
CIRCUMSTANCES ALTER CASES (84). There is a difference between,
say, six people picking blackberries in the garden and the same six
making jam of them in the kitchen.

448 Many kiss the hand they wish to cut off
Don't be deceived by mere politeness, as people are often polite
to those they intend to harm. Chaucer refers to 'the smiler with
the knife under the cloak'.
A similar proverb is FULL OF COURTESY, FULL OF CRAFT (228).

449 Many would be cowards if they had courage enough
The fact that they would be accused of cowardice if they showed
signs of it in a dangerous emergency is enough to make most people
act bravely, however scared they feel.

450 Marriage is a lottery
It all depends on the luck of the draw. One can never tell beforehand what sort of a partner one's wife or husband is going to turn
out to be.

451 Marriages are made in heaven
It is a matter of chance who marries whom. A dangerous proverb,
for if you leave your marriage entirely to chance (made in heaven)
instead of thinking intelligently about it, you increase unnecessarily
an already considerable risk.

452 Marry in haste, and repent at leisure
You will have plenty of time to regret that you were in too much
of a hurry to get married, for MARRIAGE IS A LOTTERY (450) and
WEDLOCK IS A PADLOCK (722).

**453 May God defend me from my friends; I can defend myself from
my enemies**
A tactless or blundering friend can often cause more mischief
than an enemy.
See also THERE IS SAFETY IN NUMBERS (671).

454 Men are blind in their own cause
They are so convinced that they are in the right that they can never

see things from the other person's point of view. If, for example, you are too ardently nationalistic you will become blind to the defects in your own country.

455 Men are known by the company they keep
This is simular to BIRDS OF A FEATHER FLOCK TOGETHER (54).
Benjamin Hapgood Burt, the American lyricist, wrote the following delightful jingle:

> One evening in October,
> When I was far from sober,
> And dragging home a load with manly pride,
> My feet began to stutter,
> So I laid down in the gutter,
> And a pig came up and parked right by my side.
> Then I warbled, 'It's fair weather
> When good fellows get together,'
> Till a lady passing by was heard to say:
> 'You can tell a man who boozes
> By the company he chooses.'
> And the pig got up and slowly walked away.

456 Men are not to be measured in inches
The greatness of a man does not depend on his physical stature. Napoleon Bonaparte, for example, was barely five feet two inches in height.

457 Men leap over where the hedge is lowest
It is natural in human beings to take the easiest course. There is no sense in doing things the hard way, in making difficulties for oneself.
See also CROSS THE STREAM WHERE IT IS SHALLOWEST (98).

458 Men make houses, women make homes
The husband may buy, or even build, the house, but it only becomes a real home when it is made warm and comfortable by the wife.

459 Men strain at gnats and swallow camels
This is hypocrisy, the behaviour of those who speak loudly against small offences while committing much greater offences at the same time. The source is Matthew, xxiii, 24. Jesus says to the scribes

and Pharisees: 'Ye blind guides, which strain at a gnat, and swallow a camel.' To 'strain at a gnat' is to filter the wine after finding a gnat in it.

460 Might is right
The argument put forward by those who are strong.

'It is said,' wrote Voltaire, 'that God is always on the side of the big battalions.'

Abraham Lincoln was of another opinion: 'It has been said of the world's history hitherto that might is right. It is for us and for our time to reverse the maxim, and to say that right makes might.'

461 A mill cannot grind with the water that is past
This has two meanings:

(a) The mill can be turned only by the water that is passing through it now. The water that turned it yesterday cannot be used to turn it today. The flow of time can be compared to the flow of water through the mill. We cannot use time that is past. We can use only the present time, so we must make use of our opportunities before it is too late.

(b) It is no use sighing for the past. We cannot call back happier days, but must live in the present. Nor should we allow ourselves to suffer from vain regrets. IT IS NO USE CRYING OVER SPILT MILK (366). WHAT'S DONE CANNOT BE UNDONE (729).

462 The mills of God grind slowly
This is a warning of divine retribution, which may take time but will overtake us in the end. There are various versions of it, perhaps the best known being Longfellow's:

> Though the mills of God grind slowly, yet
> they grind exceeding small;
> Though with patience He stands waiting,
> With exactness grinds he all.

463 Misfortunes never come singly
One misfortune is generally followed closely by another. As Robert Herrick wrote in his poem *Sorrows Succeed*:

> When one is past, another care we have;
> Thus woe succeeds a woe, as wave a wave.

Or, in the more modern phrase, 'Life is just one damned thing after another,' which gave John Masefield the title for his book *Odtaa*. A similar proverb is IT NEVER RAINS BUT IT POURS (372).

464   A miss is as good as a mile
Whether you have missed your objective by a narrow margin or a wide one, you have still failed. Suppose that you and your friend Douglas are among the twenty applicants for a job. Suppose that the list is whittled down until only you and Douglas remain. Suppose that Douglas is given the job. Certainly you are very unlucky, yet you are in exactly the same position as the other eighteen applicants; however narrow the margin, you have failed.

465   Moderation in all things
Moderation means avoidance of excess. Do not go to extremes.
   Similar proverbs are ENOUGH IS AS GOOD AS A FEAST (167); MORE THAN ENOUGH IS TOO MUCH (472); SAFETY LIES IN THE MIDDLE COURSE (591).

466   Money begets money
The more money you make, the easier it becomes to make still more. NOTHING SUCCEEDS LIKE SUCCESS (522).

467   Money burns a hole in the pocket
Some people spend their money so quickly that it seems as if it burns a hole in the pocket and drops out.

468   Money is the root of all evil
This is a misquotation. It is not money but the love of it that is the root of all evil.
   See THE LOVE OF MONEY IS THE ROOT OF ALL EVIL (432).

469   Money talks
Here 'talks' means 'carries weight', in the sense that it is influential. It is possible to do much more with money than without it.
   'Why did the members side with Mr X at the annual general meeting? Mr Y's arguments were much more convincing.'
   'Mr X is a rich man and Mr Y isn't. If we'd accepted Mr Y's proposals, the Club would have lost the support of Mr X. Money talks, you know.'
   See also A GOLDEN KEY OPENS EVERY DOOR (245).

470   More haste, less speed

The greater our need for haste, the more likely we are to waste time instead of saving it.

'Why does my shoelace always have to snap when I'm in a hurry?'

'It snaps *because* you're in a hurry. You get so flustered that you pull too hard on it, which makes you later than ever. More haste, less speed.'

The Latin form of this proverb was the paradox *Festina lente*, which means 'Hasten slowly'.

A similar proverb is HASTE MAKES WASTE (264).

471   More know Tom Fool than Tom Fool knows

We are known to more people than we realize.

472   More than enough is too much

This teaches moderation. It means the same thing as ENOUGH IS AS GOOD AS A FEAST (167).

Similar proverbs are MODERATION IN ALL THINGS (465); SAFETY LIES IN THE MIDDLE COURSE (591).

473   The more you have, the more you want

We are never satisfied with what we have. When we satisfy one want, it merely makes us aware of another. And so it goes on.

474   The mouse that has but one hole is quickly taken

'Consider the little mouse,' wrote Plautus, the Roman dramatist, 'how sagacious an animal it is which never entrusts his life to one hole only.' Like the sagacious mouse, we should not depend too much on one thing, but should have others in reserve. It is the same advice as given in DON'T PUT ALL YOUR EGGS IN ONE BASKET (140).

475   Much would have more

Some people, though they have a lot, are never satisfied. The ruling passion of an avaricious man is to add to his riches. Oliver Goldsmith wrote in his long poem, *The Traveller*:

> As some lone miser, visiting his store,
> Bends at his treasure, counts, re-counts it o'er;
> Hoards after hoards his rising raptures fill,
> Yet still he sighs, for hoards are wanting still.

476 Muck and money go together
You can earn good money if you don't mind dirtying your hands.
See WHERE THERE'S MUCK THERE'S BRASS (756).

477 Murder will out
It cannot be concealed indefinitely. As Dryden wrote in *The Cock and the Fox*:

> Murder may pass unpunish'd for a time,
> But tardy justice will o'ertake the crime.

See also THE TRUTH WILL OUT (699).

N

478 Nature abhors a vacuum
This idea was first expressed by Plutarch as early as the first century A.D. and is much quoted today. It means that any natural deficiency tends to be made good. Its application is, therefore, very wide indeed. Since marriage is natural, if a woman in her prime loses her husband, she will tend to marry again, as nature abhors a vacuum.

479 The nearer the church, the farther from God
This proverb springs from the idea that true religion cannot be satisfactorily organized into a church. It suggests that those most closely involved in the organization of the church are least likely to be truly religious, as they tend to become more interested in the organization than in godly living.

480 Necessity is the mother of invention
Here 'mother' means something that gives rise to something else. If we do not really need a thing, the lack of it does not trouble us, but when the need for it becomes so great that we cannot do without it, we are forced to find a way of getting it. A good example of this was the invention of radar (radio detection and ranging), a method of locating invisible objects, used first in World War II to detect the approach of enemy aircraft and submarines, and later put to many peace-time uses. Radar might never have been invented had it not been for the threat of war. Necessity was the mother of invention.

A similar proverb is WANT IS THE MOTHER OF INDUSTRY (714).

481   Necessity knows no law
The proverb could be used to justify the behaviour of a man who steals food to keep his wife and family from starving. As Cervantes wrote in *Don Quixote*: 'Necessity urges desperate measures.'

482   Needs must when the devil drives
The proverb is similar to NECESSITY KNOWS NO LAW (481), but it is also used as an excuse for not resisting temptation.

'Needs must' is used here without 'do', which completes the phrase. 'Needs must do' is synonymous with 'cannot avoid doing'.

'Why do you drink so much? You never seem to be sober.'

'I can't break myself of it. It's a question of needs must when the devil drives.'

483   Neither a borrower nor a lender be
If you borrow money from a friend you may not be able to repay it and will spoil the friendship. If you lend a friend money you may have to ask him to repay it, and this too will spoil the friendship. So neither borrow money nor lend it.

The proverb is a quotation from Shakespeare's *Hamlet*. Similar proverbs are LEND YOUR MONEY AND LOSE YOUR FRIEND (391); WHEN I LENT I HAD A FRIEND; WHEN I ASKED HE WAS UNKIND (745).

484   Never ask pardon before you are accused
Wait until you are blamed for something before you offer excuses. Otherwise you will show yourself guilty.

Martin had had a very trying day at the office. Nothing had gone right, and he was still not in the best of tempers when he met Sarah at the café in the evening. After a time Sarah became worried by his moody silence.

'What's the matter, Martin?' she asked.

'Nothing.'

'It's not anything I've done, is it?'

'How do you mean?'

'Well, you're not cross because I went to the pictures with Clive Long last night, are you?'

'I didn't know you did, but thanks for telling me.'

And that was how the row started.

485   Never buy a pig in a poke

Always examine your purchase before you pay for it. A poke is a bag or sack. In olden days a crafty trader would tie a cat in a sack and sell it to some trusting simpleton as a piglet, much more valuable than a mere cat. If the would-be buyer was wise enough to insist on seeing the piglet before parting with his money, the trader's dishonesty would be revealed. Hence the proverbial expression 'to let the cat out of the bag', which means, in a figurative sense, to give away a secret.

486   Never do things by halves

Finish a thing once you have started it. Do all that is necessary to make a good job of it, and don't work in a half-hearted way. IF A THING IS WORTH DOING IT IS WORTH DOING WELL (319).

487   Never judge by appearances

Never base your opinion of anything merely on what it looks like, for APPEARANCES ARE DECEPTIVE (19) and THINGS ARE SELDOM WHAT THEY SEEM (677). For example, we must crack an egg before we can be sure that it is good or bad.

Other proverbs that teach us the same lesson are ALL THAT GLITTERS IS NOT GOLD (15) and THE COWL DOES NOT MAKE THE MONK (96). See also ALL ARE NOT THIEVES THAT DOGS BARK AT (7); FINE FEATHERS MAKE FINE BIRDS (206); THE TAILOR MAKES THE MAN (630).

488   Never look a gift horse in the mouth

Never be too critical of anything you have received as a gift.

The condition of a horse's teeth is a good guide to its age. If a man needs a horse and is offered one for nothing, he should not examine its teeth too closely before accepting it.

Here is an example of how the proverb is used:

'My uncle has bought himself a new car and has given me his old one, but it rattles like mad and won't do more than forty-five.'

'It's better than no car at all, though, isn't it?'

'Oh, yes.'

'Then don't look a gift horse in the mouth.'

Similar proverbs are BEGGARS MUST NOT BE CHOOSERS (37); HE WHO PAYS THE PIPER CALLS THE TUNE (293).

489 Never make threats you cannot carry out
This is sound advice because, if your bluff is called, you look very silly.
A similar proverb is IF YOU CANNOT BITE NEVER SHOW YOUR TEETH (331).

490 Never make two bites of a cherry
If a job can be done in one short spell of work, don't break off and come back to it later.

491 Never put off till tomorrow what may be done today
If a thing has to be done, do it now. Remember that PROCRASTINATION IS THE THIEF OF TIME (567).
Similar proverbs are GATHER YE ROSEBUDS WHILE YE MAY (229); MAKE HAY WHILE THE SUN SHINES (436); ONE OF THESE DAYS IS NONE OF THESE DAYS (538); STRIKE WHILE THE IRON IS HOT (624); TAKE TIME BY THE FORELOCK (639); TOMORROW NEVER COMES (692); WHAT MAY BE DONE AT ANY TIME IS DONE AT NO TIME (735).

492 Never say die
Never give up. While there's life there's hope. Press on!

493 Never spend your money before you have it
This teaches prudence. If your uncle promises to give you fifty pounds on your twenty-first birthday, which is in six months' time, don't borrow money on the strength of it. It is not that you do not trust your uncle to keep his promise, but anything may happen in the meantime and you *may* be faced with a debt that you cannot repay.
Similar proverbs are CATCH YOUR BEAR BEFORE YOU SELL ITS SKIN (76); DON'T COUNT YOUR CHICKENS BEFORE THEY ARE HATCHED (124); DO NOT HALLOO TILL YOU ARE OUT OF THE WOOD (131); FIRST CATCH YOUR HARE (210); THERE'S MANY A SLIP 'TWIXT THE CUP AND THE LIP (655).

494 Never spur a willing horse
A 'willing horse' is a person who works well and without complaint (ALL LAY LOADS ON A WILLING HORSE (13)). Don't urge him on to work harder and faster, for he may then do less, or not be quite so willing.

495   Never tell your enemy that your foot aches
Never admit a weakness to a person who is liable to take advantage of it.

A similar proverb is IT IS A FOOLISH SHEEP THAT MAKES THE WOLF HIS CONFESSOR (348).

496   Never trouble trouble till trouble troubles you
Never look for trouble. Don't worry about something before it has happened. Your fears may be groundless, for it may never happen.

Mr King was driving his wife to the airport.

'I'm terrified we shan't get there in time,' she said anxiously. 'Supposing the car breaks down or we skid into a lamp-post or run over a dog?'

'For heaven's sake stop worrying!' he replied. 'We're all right so far, aren't we?'

'Yes, but—'

'Then keep quiet and let me get on with the driving.'

Mrs King caught the plane.

Similar proverbs are DON'T CROSS A BRIDGE TILL YOU COME TO IT (125); DON'T CRY BEFORE YOU ARE HURT (126); DON'T MEET TROUBLE HALF-WAY (137); SUFFICIENT UNTO THE DAY IS THE EVIL THEREOF (627).

497   New brooms sweep clean
People newly appointed to posts tend to make big changes. Like new brooms, they do their work thoroughly.

When Mrs Bristow retired, Miss Parsons was appointed superintendent of the department. She found fault with all Mrs Bristow's methods, which she described as old-fashioned, and turned the department upside down, much to the annoyance of the girls who had worked so happily under Mrs Bristow. Little wonder they muttered among themselves about new brooms!

498   Ninety per cent of inspiration is perspiration
The dictionary tells us that inspiration is 'divine influence, especially that which is thought to visit poets etc.' But although inspiration supplies the ideas, these have to be put into words, which is the most difficult part of it. Inspiration is useless without an aptitude for hard work; hence the perspiration!

499   No answer is also an answer

If you ask a person a question and he does not reply, his very silence is an answer in itself.

'Have you been playing about with my typewriter?' demanded young Tommy's sister.

He pretended to be deep in the book he was reading. She did not ask him a second time because she knew that he had been tampering with the machine and did not want to admit it.

A somewhat similar proverb is SILENCE GIVES CONSENT (601).

500   No cross, no crown

Just as Christ could not achieve the Kingdom of Heaven without suffering crucifixion (on the Cross), so no one can expect to achieve anything worth while without pain.

Similar proverbs are NO GAIN WITHOUT PAIN (501); THERE IS NO PLEASURE WITHOUT PAIN (662); THROUGH HARDSHIP TO THE STARS (682).

501   No gain without pain

This is a milder version of NO CROSS, NO CROWN (500) and means simply that you are unlikely to achieve anything without some trouble or hardship.

502   No man can serve two masters

A man with two employers cannot be faithful to both. Nor can a man support two conflicting causes. The source is Matthew, vi, 24: 'No man can serve two masters; for either he will hate the one, and love the other; or else he will hold to the one, and despise the other. Ye cannot serve God and mammon.'

Other proverbs on the theme of 'either – or' are A DOOR MUST BE EITHER SHUT OR OPEN (152); YOU CANNOT BURN THE CANDLE AT BOTH ENDS (777); YOU CANNOT HAVE IT BOTH WAYS (781); YOU CANNOT HAVE YOUR CAKE AND EAT IT (782); YOU CANNOT RUN WITH THE HARE AND HUNT WITH THE HOUNDS (788); YOU CANNOT SELL THE COW AND DRINK THE MILK (789).

503   No man is a hero to his valet

A valet is a manservant who attends to his master's person and to his clothes. He knows more about his master than anyone else does, since his master can keep nothing secret from him. Thus no one is more aware than the valet that his master has human failings.

See also FAMILIARITY BREEDS CONTEMPT (203); RESPECT IS GREATER FROM A DISTANCE (583).

504 No man is content with his lot
Here 'lot' means 'condition', 'share of worldly reward'. We are none of us satisfied with the way we have to live and the work we have to do.

505 No man is indispensable
This is a proverb used often in business organizations.

'How we're going to get along without Mr Kennett I just can't imagine.'

'We'll manage all right. No man is indispensable.'

506 No man is infallible
All of us are liable to make mistakes now and then. TO ERR IS HUMAN (690) and EVEN HOMER SOMETIMES NODS (169).

507 No names, no pack drill
Don't mention names in case anyone suffers.

This is an Army saying. Pack drill is a form of punishment for offences against military discipline. Should a soldier have committed such an offence, and the authorities be unable to find out who did it, he will probably escape pack drill if all his comrades pretend complete ignorance of the matter.

A proverb that is very similar is DON'T TELL TALES OUT OF SCHOOL (148).

508 No news is good news
Bad news is an urgent matter and people usually write off at once to tell their relatives or friends. Good news, of course, can be just as important sometimes ('It's a boy!'), but if we receive no news at all, we can safely assume that all is well.

'We've heard nothing from Cousin Maud for nearly a year. I hope she's all right.'

'Don't worry, dear. She's probably been too busy to write to us. No news is good news.'

509   Noblesse oblige

This is one of those proverbs that have remained more common in their original form than in the English translation. It is the French for 'Birth compels it', which means that noble birth imposes the obligation of noble actions.

510   A nod is as good as a wink

It is sometimes better to avoid putting thoughts into words. A slight change of expression on a person's face should be enough to convey his meaning.

'Wilson didn't actually say so, but a nod's as good as a wink and we can safely assume that he thinks the same about that solicitor fellow as we do.'

A somewhat similar proverb is A WORD IS ENOUGH TO THE WISE (770).

511   A nod is as good as a wink to a blind horse

It is no use giving a hint to a person who is determined not to take it.

Similar proverbs are NONE SO BLIND AS THOSE WHO WON'T SEE (513); NONE SO DEAF AS THOSE WHO WON'T HEAR (514).

512   None but the brave deserves the fair

You have to act boldly to win the girl you love, for FAINT HEART NE'ER WON FAIR LADY (201). Other proverbs teaching self-confidence are FORTUNE FAVOURS THE BOLD (224); HE WHO HESITATES IS LOST (291); NOTHING VENTURE, NOTHING HAVE (523).

513   None so blind as those who won't see

It is no use trying to get a person to see what he does not wish to see, or to understand what he chooses not to understand, or to attract his attention when he has decided to ignore you.

'I've been trying to catch his eye ever since he came into the hall, but he's always looking some other way.'

'There's none so blind as those who won't see.'

A similar proverb is A NOD IS AS GOOD AS A WINK TO A BLIND HORSE (511).

514   None so deaf as those who won't hear

Just as it is no use trying to get a person to see what he does not wish to see, so is it useless to persuade a person to hear what he does not wish to hear.

Mr Harris strode down to the bottom of the garden, where his son was busy doing nothing among the bushes.

'Why don't you come in when I call you?' he demanded.

'I'm sorry, Dad, but I didn't hear you.'

'None so deaf as those who won't hear. Get back indoors and do your homework.'

515 Not good is it to harp on the frayed string

Don't keep on talking about the same thing or bringing up the same subject. Literally 'to harp' is to play the harp; figuratively 'to harp on' is to dwell tediously on a matter. Here 'frayed' means that the harp-string (and the subject) is becoming worn out through too much use.

Similar proverbs are DON'T TAKE YOUR HARP TO THE PARTY (146); HARP NOT FOR EVER ON THE SAME STRING (263); IT IS USELESS TO FLOG A DEAD HORSE (370).

516 Nothing is as good as it seems beforehand

This means the same as EXPECTATION IS BETTER THAN REALIZATION (195).

517 Nothing is given so freely as advice

Although most of us do not welcome advice, we are all only too ready to give it.

518 Nothing is so certain as the unexpected

This means the same as IT IS THE UNEXPECTED THAT ALWAYS HAPPENS (368).

519 Nothing seek, nothing find

This teaches initiative. Success is not achieved without an effort. 'He that seeketh findeth,' runs the old saying, and in Matthew vii, 7 we read: 'Seek and ye shall find; knock and it shall be opened unto you.'

If you are looking for a job, don't wait for somebody to offer you one, but go out and look for it yourself.

520 Nothing so bad but might have been worse

There is always something to be thankful for.

'The house was burnt to the ground, but things might have been worse, for I managed to save the manuscript of the book I'd just finished. Think of having to write that all over again!'

A similar proverb is EVERY CLOUD HAS A SILVER LINING (171).

521 Nothing stake, nothing draw

This refers to gambling. If you are not prepared to stake any money, you cannot expect to win any. In a wider sense this means the same as NOTHING VENTURE, NOTHING HAVE (523).

522 Nothing succeeds like success

It is not easy to achieve success, but once you have achieved it, the way is open to even greater prosperity. For example, a novelist, may write nine books and yet remain comparatively unknown. Then the tenth book becomes a best-seller, which not only ensures success for any further books he may write but also creates a demand for the first nine.

See also MONEY BEGETS MONEY (466).

523 Nothing venture, nothing have

This advises bold action. If you are not prepared to take risks, you cannot expect to get results.

'I want to borrow the car for the week-end, but I don't think Dad will let me have it.'

'Go and ask him. Nothing venture, nothing have.'

Similar proverbs are: NOTHING STAKE, NOTHING DRAW (521); FORTUNE FAVOURS THE BOLD (224).

O

524 Of two evils choose the lesser

'When compelled to choose one of two evils,' wrote Socrates, 'no one will choose the greater when he may choose the lesser.' Charles H. Spurgeon, the great Baptist minister, took a stronger view: 'Of two evils, choose neither.'

Current usage of the proverb is fairly light-hearted. For example: 'I either had to walk the two miles to the station or ask old Jessop to give me a lift. As he's the worst driver I've ever met, I chose the lesser of two evils and walked.'

525 An old poacher makes the best keeper
He knows all the tricks of poaching, so is best fitted to deal with other poachers. A similar proverb is SET A THIEF TO CATCH A THIEF (598).

526 Once bitten, twice shy
If we have had an unpleasant experience, we are very anxious to avoid a repetition.

'Mr Saunders,' said the schoolmistress, 'we are taking another party of children up to see the sights of London next Saturday. Would you like to help us as you so kindly did last time?'

'I'm sorry, Miss Osborne, but I'd much rather not,' he replied. 'Those infernal kids nearly drove me mad. "Once bitten, twice shy" is my motto from now on.'

A similar proverb is A BURNT CHILD DREADS THE FIRE (65).

527 One beats the bush, and another catches the birds
One man does all the hard work, and another reaps the benefit. The reference is to the beater, whose job it is to strike the bushes and rouse the birds or other game so that the sportsman with the gun can take a shot at them.

See also ONE MAN SOWS AND ANOTHER REAPS (534).

528 One cannot be in two places at once
This axiom is often used as an excuse for not doing something.

529 One cannot put back the clock
This is a reminder to the reactionary who dreams of the 'good old days' and would like to see them again. He should realize that TIMES CHANGE (689).

530 One foot is better than two crutches
This means the same as HALF A LOAF IS BETTER THAN NO BREAD (258). We should be thankful for what we have, even though it is less than we would like.

531 One good turn deserves another
If someone has done you a kindness, you should do him a kindness in return.

A boy was once able to help a circus elephant by stopping another boy from throwing stones at it. A year later the circus again visited the town, and while the elephant was doing his tricks in the ring he caught sight of his benefactor sitting on a hard form. He immediately broke off his performance, lifted the boy up in his trunk and placed him carefully down in a plush-covered seat in the most expensive part of the marquee.

An elephant never forgets, and one good turn deserves another. GIVE AND TAKE (233).

532   One is never too old to learn

However much you know, there is always more to learn, and whatever your age, you can still increase your knowledge. Cicero refers to 'a zeal of learning, which, in the case of wise and well-trained men, advances in every pace with age'. The favourite saying of Michelangelo, the great Italian sculptor and painter, was: 'I am learning.'

533   One lie makes many

The telling of one lie forces us to tell more lies, and so we become more and more deeply involved.

See also LIARS SHOULD HAVE GOOD MEMORIES (402).

534   One man sows and another reaps

One man does the work and another gets the benefit. A similar proverb is ONE BEATS THE BUSH, AND ANOTHER CATCHES THE BIRDS (527).

535   One man's meat is another man's poison

Food that agrees with one person may have an injurious effect on another. In a wider sense one person may like what another hates.

'My sister loves cowboy films on TV, but I can't stand them.'

'Don't forget the old saying, "One man's meat is another man's poison." '

Similar proverbs are BEAUTY IS IN THE EYE OF THE BEHOLDER (36); EVERYONE TO HIS TASTE (188); TASTES DIFFER (642); THERE IS NO DISPUTING ABOUT TASTES (657).

536   One must draw back in order to leap better

This teaches prudence. It is a quotation from an essay by Montaigne ('Il faut reculer pour mieux sauter') and has much the same meaning as LOOK BEFORE YOU LEAP (426), except that the stress is not on looking but on making previous preparations. For example, a stream may be too wide for us to clear in one leap from a standing position on the bank. We therefore withdraw several paces so that a preliminary run will give us the necessary impetus to reach the other side. In the same way, it is not wise, even though we are in a hurry, to embark on something without previous thought and planning, which may seem to be slowing us down, but in fact hastens our progress.

537   One must draw the line somewhere
To draw the line is to lay down a definite limit of action beyond which one refuses to go. The decision depends on ourselves, but it must be taken sooner or later.

'My wife and I were getting so many invitations to dinner parties that we never had an evening to ourselves. We had to draw the line somewhere, so now we turn down all invitations for Tuesdays and Thursdays.'

538   One of these days is none of these days
'I'll do it one of these days.' This means that you propose to do whatever it is later on. The result is that it is never done at all. PROCRASTINATION IS THE THIEF OF TIME (567).

Similar proverbs are GATHER YE ROSEBUDS WHILE YE MAY (229); MAKE HAY WHILE THE SUN SHINES (436); NEVER PUT OFF TILL TOMORROW WHAT MAY BE DONE TODAY (491); STRIKE WHILE THE IRON IS HOT (624); TAKE TIME BY THE FORELOCK (639); TOMORROW NEVER COMES (692); WHAT MAY BE DONE AT ANY TIME IS DONE AT NO TIME (735).

539   One pair of heels is often worth two pairs of hands
Usage associates heels with running. To take to one's heels is to make a hasty departure. This proverb, therefore, means that it is often better to run away than to stop and fight.

Similar proverbs are BETTER BEND THAN BREAK (47); DIS-CRETION IS THE BETTER PART OF VALOUR (117); HE THAT FIGHTS AND RUNS AWAY MAY LIVE TO FIGHT ANOTHER DAY (273).

540   One swallow does not make a summer
The swallow is a migratory bird, visiting Great Britain in April

and leaving for warmer climes in September. As far as Great
Britain is concerned, 'spring' is more accurate than 'summer'.
Aristotle, the Greek philosopher, wrote: 'One swallow does not
make spring, nor does one fine day.'

The proverb reminds us that winter is not necessarily over just
because we have seen one swallow. By extension we are reminded
also that any single piece of evidence is not enough to prove
anything. It may even be an exception.

541   One touch of nature makes the whole world kin
In general usage this proverb means that the show of a funda-
mental human emotion, or even human weakness, often has the
effect of bringing people closer together.

The quotation comes from Shakespeare's tragedy, *Troilus and
Cressida*.

542   One volunteer is worth two pressed men
Here 'pressed' means 'compelled to serve in the armed forces'.
The modern term is 'conscripted' or 'called up'. A volunteer joins
of his own free will and so is much more likely than a pressed man
to be an efficient sailor or soldier. The same applies in a wider
sense. Mr James, Mr Turner and Mr Roberts were all members of
the committee of the Tennis Club. Mr Turner had offered his
services; the other two had been 'talked into it', persuaded against
their wishes. What happened? Mr Turner did more useful work
for the Tennis Club than the other two put together.

543   Only the wearer knows where the shoe pinches
No one except he who is experiencing it knows the cause of a
trouble or difficulty. His behaviour is not understood by others
because they are unaware of the motive behind it. For example,
a man resigned from a highly paid post in a business organization
for no apparent reason, and everyone wondered why. The truth
was that the managing director's wife had fallen in love with him,
which had caused him so much embarrassment that the only way
to avoid her was to seek employment elsewhere.

544   Open confession is good for the soul
A guilty secret is hard to bear; it has a bad effect on us. The more
we try to forget it, the more we are reminded of it. But once we
have openly confessed it and brought it out into the open, we are

happy again and mentally at peace. Confession can be described as a medicine that heals the mind.

A similar proverb is A FAULT CONFESSED IS HALF REDRESSED (204).

545 Opportunity makes the thief

If you leave articles of value lying about, you are asking for them to be stolen. The temptation may be too great for a person who would not otherwise have thought to steal, so your carelessness has brought another thief into the world.

546 Opportunity seldom knocks twice

Another proverb tells us that FORTUNE KNOCKS AT LEAST ONCE AT EVERY MAN'S GATE (225), but that does not necessarily mean that it will knock a second time, so when an opportunity to do a thing on which you have set your heart does suddenly arise you should take full advantage of it, for you may never get another chance.

For other proverbs on the theme of opportunity see GATHER YE ROSEBUDS WHILE YE MAY (229); HE THAT WILL NOT WHEN HE MAY, WHEN HE WILL HE SHALL HAVE NAY (280); HE WHO HESITATES IS LOST (291); HOIST YOUR SAIL WHEN THE WIND IS FAIR (308); LIFE IS SHORT AND TIME IS SWIFT (404); MAKE HAY WHILE THE SUN SHINES (436); STRIKE WHILE THE IRON IS HOT (624); THERE IS A TIDE IN THE AFFAIRS OF MEN . . . (651); TIME AND TIDE WAIT FOR NO MAN (685).

547 Other times, other manners

Each succeeding generation has its own way of life and standard of behaviour.

548 An ounce of discretion is worth a pound of wit

Don't try to be too funny at other people's expense. Your jokes may pain them or give offence.

549 Out of debt, out of danger

There are considerable risks attached to being in debt, for a man without money is so defenceless. Once he has paid off his debts and has begun to build up a balance at the bank, he is in a much safer position.

550   Out of sight, out of mind
We cease to worry about anything that can no longer be seen. This includes people. Absent friends are soon forgotten. This is the opposite of ABSENCE MAKES THE HEART GROW FONDER (1).

P

551   Paddle your own canoe
Do it yourself. Don't always expect others to help you. Be self-reliant.

552   Patience is a virtue
It is also the art of hoping. We must be patient and not despair. See also THEY ALSO SERVE WHO ONLY STAND AND WAIT (672).

553   The pen is mightier than the sword
The written word is more to be feared than physical force. 'Tyranny has no enemy as formidable as the pen,' wrote William Cobbett, and John Taylor gave us this:

> Pens are most dangerous tools, more sharp by odds
> Than swords, and cut more keen than whips or rods.

As a commentary on the 1960s it can be suggested that although the pen is mightier than the sword, even mightier than the pen is television.

A similar proverb is THE TONGUE IS NOT STEEL, YET IT CUTS (694).

554   Per ardua ad astra
This is one of those proverbs that have remained more common in their original form than in their English translation, mainly because it is the motto of the Royal Air Force. It is the Latin for THROUGH HARDSHIP TO THE STARS (682). An alternative version in Latin is *Per aspera ad astra*.

555   The pitcher goes so often to the well that it is broken at last
This means that long-continued success ends at length in failure; and that long-continued impunity ends at length in punishment.

However many times an action is performed, it will be done once too often; and however many times a swindler, trickster or thief succeeds, he will finally get caught out.

556   A place for everything, and everything in its place
This was quoted by Emerson in his *Journal* in 1857. We find it also in *Thrift* by Samuel Smiles (1875). The proverb recommends tidiness. Everything has its proper place, and when it is to be found there when it is needed, life goes more smoothly.

557   Pleasant hours fly fast
When we are enjoying ourselves, time passes far too quickly, but it passes very slowly when we are bored, or have nothing to do, or are working on some uncongenial task. Then we can use the other old proverb, A WATCHED POT NEVER BOILS (716).

558   Possession is nine points of the law
We use this to mean that even though full legal right to a thing has not been established, he who is in possession of it has a far greater right to it than has anybody else.

The original meaning (seventeenth century) was rather different. If in a legal action to establish the ownership of property – say a piece of land – neither side was able to establish title (written proof of right), certain points had to be settled before a decision could be reached. Sometimes there were twelve of these, sometimes ten, and it was more than likely that most of them would be settled in favour of the person who was in actual possession of the property.

559   The pot called the kettle black
A person tends to blame another for the faults he has himself.

The soot from an open fire blackens the cooking utensils placed upon it, and the pot becomes no less blackened than the kettle. It has, therefore, no right to criticize the kettle, and neither have we the right to condemn others for behaving in the same way as we do ourselves.

Mr Hardwick was standing at the window of his office when his visitor arrived.

'See those workmen over there?' he said. 'They're supposed to be mending the road, but they've been standing round doing nothing for half an hour. I know that for a fact, because I've been watching them.'

'Really?' said the visitor. 'And how much work have *you* been doing during that half-hour? Talk about the pot calling the kettle black!'

560 Pouring oil on the fire is not the way to quench it

If you wish to pacify a man who has lost his temper, don't say anything that is likely to make him angrier than ever.

561 Poverty is no sin

It is not a crime to be poor. That, however, does not make it any easier to put up with. 'Poverty is no disgrace to a man,' said Sydney Smith, that eminent and witty cleric of a former generation, 'but it is confoundedly inconvenient.'

562 Practice makes perfect

Only by doing a thing again and again can you attain skill or efficiency. A professional juggler does not learn to balance three billiards balls on the tip of his nose by watching others perform. He must do it himself and go on doing it, despite constant failures until he can do it without error.

Similar proverbs are ALL THINGS ARE DIFFICULT BEFORE THEY ARE EASY (16); IF AT FIRST YOU DON'T SUCCEED, TRY, TRY, TRY AGAIN (320); LEARN TO WALK BEFORE YOU RUN (389).

563 Practise what you preach

Here 'practise' means 'carry out in action'. The moral is: Behave in the same way as you advise others to behave. Do not recommend early rising if you yourself lie in bed till noon.

'Don't keep on sniffing, Johnny,' said his sister. 'Blow your nose.'

'You're a one to talk!' exclaimed Johnny. 'You sniff more than I do. Practise what you preach!'

See also EXAMPLE IS BETTER THAN PRECEPT (192).

564 Praise makes good men better and bad men worse

Praise is encouragement, so to praise a good man is to encourage him in rectitude, and to praise a bad man is to encourage him in wickedness.

565 Praise without profit puts little in the pot

Flattery does not fill the belly, and when people speak kindly of what you have done, it is of no real advantage to you unless they show their appreciation in a more material way.

Similar proverbs are ACTIONS SPEAK LOUDER THAN WORDS (3); FINE WORDS BUTTER NO PARSNIPS (207); HE WHO GIVES FAIR WORDS FEEDS YOU WITH AN EMPTY SPOON (288).

566 Prevention is better than cure
It is better to take precautions against a thing happening than to have to repair the damage after it has occurred. For example, if a bicycle tyre is badly worn it is better to have a new one fitted than take the chance of a blow-out when you are miles from anywhere.

567 Procrastination is the thief of time
To procrastinate is to delay, to put off doing something. Procrastinating – deferring things from day to day – wastes a lot of time and usually ends in nothing being done at all.

The proverb is a quotation from the poem *Night Thoughts*, by Edward Young.

Similar proverbs are GATHER YE ROSEBUDS WHILE YE MAY (229); MAKE HAY WHILE THE SUN SHINES (436); NEVER PUT OFF TILL TOMORROW WHAT MAY BE DONE TODAY (491); ONE OF THESE DAYS IS NONE OF THESE DAYS (538); STRIKE WHILE THE IRON IS HOT (624); TAKE TIME BY THE FORELOCK (639); THERE IS NO TIME LIKE THE PRESENT (666); TOMORROW NEVER COMES (692); WHAT MAY BE DONE AT ANY TIME IS DONE AT NO TIME (735).

568 Promises are like pie-crust, made to be broken
That is the trouble with promises; so often they are made and never kept. 'A man apt to promise,' wrote Thomas Fuller, 'is apt to forget.'

Pie-crust is the baked paste forming the crust of a pie. Its only purpose is to be cooked and eaten with the pie.

569 The proof of the pudding is in the eating
A pudding is intended for only one purpose: to be eaten. Only by eating it can we prove its excellence – or lack of it. In the same way, we cannot judge the wisdom or prudence of any action until it has been put into practice.

'Our young friend Michael seems to be taking a big risk by starting up in business on his own. Isn't that asking for trouble?'

'It's hard to say yet. He's just as likely to make a success of it. After all, the proof of the pudding is in the eating, isn't it?'

570   The proper study of mankind is man
Taken from Pope's *Essay on Man* (1733), this means that our thinking and study should be devoted primarily to understanding and improving the condition of man.

571   A prophet is not without honour, save in his own country, and in his own house
A man's abilities are seldom recognized by his family and others who know him well.

The source is Matthew, xiii, 57. Here is the story as told in the New English Bible:

When he had finished these parables Jesus left that place, and came to his home town, where he taught the people in their synagogue. In amazement they asked, 'Where does he get this wisdom from, and these miraculous powers? Is he not the carpenter's son? Is not his mother called Mary, his brothers James, Joseph, Simon, and Judas? And are not all his sisters here with us? Where then has he got all this from?' So they fell foul of him, and this led him to say, 'A prophet will always be held in honour, except in his home town, and in his own family.' And he did not work many miracles there; such was their want of faith.

See also FAMILIARITY BREEDS CONTEMPT (203); RESPECT IS GREATER FROM A DISTANCE (583).

572   Prosperity makes friends, adversity tries them
It is not until a rich man has come down in the world that he knows who are his real friends.

See also is A FRIEND IN NEED IS A FRIEND INDEED (226).

573   Providence is always on the side of the big battalions
This means the same as GOD IS ALWAYS ON THE SIDE OF THE BIG BATTALIONS (240), which is also referred to under MIGHT IS RIGHT (460).

574   Punctuality is the politeness of kings
It is very important to be punctual and it is very rude to be unpunctual.

Sometimes 'princes' is used instead of 'kings'. The version above was the saying of King Louis XVIII of France. 'And,' added Samuel Smiles in his famous book, *Self Help*, 'it is also the duty of gentlemen, and the necessity of men of business.'

Some more notes on punctuality are given under BETTER LATE THAN NEVER (48).

575 The purse of the patient protracts the disease

If a doctor receives a fee for every visit, and should the patient have plenty of money, the doctor may be tempted to ensure that the patient does not get well too quickly. The same applies in other walks of life:

'He's giving me ten bob an hour, so I'm making the job last out.'

576 Put the saddle on the right horse

Blame those who deserve it, not those who don't.

An author's new book had been reviewed unfavourably in a literary weekly. He said to an acquaintance:

'I'll concede that a critic has a right to give an honest opinion, but I think John Cartright went a bit too far this time.'

'How do you know it was Cartright? The article wasn't signed.'

'I'd recognize his style anywhere, confound him!'

'You're putting the saddle on the wrong horse, old man. John Cartright didn't write that review. *I* did.'

Q

577 Queen Anne is dead

A sarcastic way of saying: 'That's old news. I heard it weeks ago.'

R

578 Rain before seven, fine before eleven

This piece of optimism is based on the weather in Britain, where early-morning rain sometimes gives way to fine weather later in the day. The proverb is occasionally applied to other situations where it is hoped that things will improve after a bad start.

579   Rats desert a sinking ship
We use this proverb in referring to those who are the first to seek
safety when danger threatens, or to fade away at the first sign of
trouble.

580   The receiver is as bad as the thief
If a man buys or otherwise acquires anything that he knows has
been stolen, he is as guilty as the person who stole it. In the same
way, if one man slanders another, he cannot excuse himself by
saying that he has merely repeated what other people have said.

581   Red sky at night . . .
>   Red sky at night, shepherd's delight:
>   Red sky in the morning, shepherd's warning.

A piece of weather lore that dates back to the sixteenth century,
this is reasonably true for other countries besides Britain, as a
very red sunset is usually followed by a fine day, whilst a very red
sunrise often foretells a break in the weather.

582   The remedy may be worse than the disease
Measures to deal with evils of one kind or another often make the
situation worse. For example, calling in the armed forces during
a period of public unrest is liable to make the remedy worse than
the disease if it is done too hurriedly.

583   Respect is greater from a distance
A man who keeps himself apart from other people is more likely
to be held in general esteem than one who lowers himself by
mixing with Tom, Dick and Harry. FAMILIARITY BREEDS CON-
TEMPT (203).

584   Revenge is sweet
This has been described as 'a devilish phrase in the mouth of men'.
Milton wrote in *Paradise Lost*:
>   Revenge, at first though sweet,
>   Bitter ere long back on itself recoils.

See also AN EYE FOR AN EYE, AND A TOOTH FOR A TOOTH (199).

585 A rich man's joke is always funny

> Money is honey, my little sonny,
> And a rich man's joke is always funny.

This couplet was written by Thomas Edward Brown, the Manx poet. The rich man's joke may not be a very good one but it is always laughed at by the flatterers and yes-men who surround him. The poor man on the edge of the crowd around the rich man may tell better jokes, but nobody listens to him.

586 The road to hell is paved with good intentions

When not followed by good deeds, good intentions are worse than useless, and the more often we fail to turn our good intentions into actuality, the worse is the effect on our characters. We become less and less able to keep our good resolutions and sink lower and lower in our downward course – the road that leads to hell.

587 A rolling stone gathers no moss

This is a very famous proverb. It means that a person who never stops long in one place, or is constantly changing his job, will never make money. It can also be used in reference to people whose love affairs are so casual and frequent that they gain no real or enduring affection.

588 Rome was not built in a day

This proverb teaches patience and perseverance. Important tasks call for a lot of hard work and take a long time to complete. Often the proverb is used as an excuse for delay.

'Haven't you finished mowing the lawn yet?' complained Mrs Nagg.

Her husband mopped his brow with his handkerchief.

'Give me time,' he answered. 'Rome wasn't built in a day.'

Other proverbs on the theme of perseverence are CONSTANT DRIPPING WEARS AWAY THE STONE (90); IF AT FIRST YOU DON'T SUCCEED, TRY, TRY, TRY AGAIN (320); IT'S DOGGED THAT DOES IT (356); LITTLE BY LITTLE AND BIT BY BIT (415); LITTLE STROKES FELL GREAT OAKS (419); SLOW BUT SURE WINS THE RACE (603); WHERE THERE'S A WILL THERE'S A WAY (755).

589   A rose by any other name would smell as sweet
It is not what a thing is called that matters, but what it *is*. The
same applies to people.

The quotation comes from Shakespeare's tragedy, *Romeo and
Juliet*. The two chief families in Verona, the Capulets and the
Montagues, are long-standing enemies. Romeo, who is a Mon-
tague, falls in love with Juliet, who is a Capulet, and she with him.
Knowing that there can be no marriage between the two houses,
Juliet laments that she was born a Capulet and he a Montague.

> 'Tis but thy name that is my enemy . . .
> What's in a name? that which we call a rose
> By any other name would smell as sweet.

590   The rotten apple injures its neighbours
One person can have a very bad influence on others. Similar
proverbs dealing with the dangers of keeping bad company are
HE SHOULD HAVE A LONG SPOON THAT SUPS WITH THE DEVIL
(270); HE THAT TOUCHETH PITCH SHALL BE DEFILED (279); WHO
KEEPS COMPANY WITH THE WOLF WILL LEARN TO HOWL (762).

S

591   Safety lies in the middle course
Do not go to extremes. Always compromise if that is possible.

Similar proverbs are ENOUGH IS AS GOOD AS A FEAST (167);
MODERATION IN ALL THINGS (465); MORE THAN ENOUGH IS TOO
MUCH (472).

592   Saying is one thing and doing another
This means the same as EASIER SAID THAN DONE (158).

593   Second thoughts are best
To have second thoughts is to reconsider a matter, and we usually
find that our second decision is wiser than the first.

'I was just sitting down to write him a strong letter of complaint
when I had second thoughts and went round to see him instead.
We parted the best of friends.'

594   Seeing is believing
Many people are reluctant to believe a thing unless they can see it.

595 Self-praise is no recommendation
You may be proud of your achievements; you may have a very
high opinion of yourself; you may think that others should be
made to realize what a fine fellow you are. But nobody will ever
have a high opinion of you if you have too high an opinion of
yourself, because a person who praises himself is never believed.

'I admit I didn't score any of the goals, but it was largely due
to me that we won the game.'

'Self-praise is no recommendation.'

596 Self-preservation is the first law of nature
We often use this as an excuse for our own selfish conduct – for
'looking after number one'. See also EVERY MAN FOR HIMSELF,
AND THE DEVIL TAKE THE HINDMOST (180).

597 Set a beggar on horseback and he'll ride to the devil
When a man without money grows suddenly rich, he is liable to
become the most arrogant of mortals. John Wolcot, whose pen-
name was Peter Pindar, wrote in his *Epistle to Lord Lonsdale*:

> Such is the bad effect of wealth – rank pride –
> Mount but a beggar, how the rogue will ride!

The term 'beggar on horseback' is used to describe an upstart,
one who has suddenly gone up in the world and has no manners.

598 Set a thief to catch a thief
A thief knows all the tricks of the game, so is best fitted to catch
others engaged in it. A similar proverb is AN OLD POACHER
MAKES THE BEST KEEPER (525). Thomas Fuller wrote in his
Church History of Britain (1655): 'Always set a thief to catch a
thief; the greatest deer-stalkers make the best park-keepers.'

599 Share and share alike
Those engaged in any joint enterprise should divide the profits (or
losses) fairly.

600 The shortest way round is the longest way home
Short cuts can involve one in difficulties. See THE LONGEST WAY
ROUND IS THE NEAREST WAY HOME (425).

601   Silence gives consent

If a person disagrees with something, or is unwilling to do as requested, he usually says so. If he makes no protest at the time, we assume that he has no objection. Thus no one can absolve himself from blame by saying nothing.

A somewhat similar proverb is NO ANSWER IS ALSO AN ANSWER (499). See also THERE IS A SIN OF OMISSION AS WELL AS OF COMMISSION (650).

602   Silence is golden

See SPEECH IS SILVER, SILENCE IS GOLDEN (613).

603   Slow but sure wins the race

This refers to the fable of the hare and the tortoise. The race was won by the slow tortoise, which plodded steadily on while the fast hare, confident of victory, took things too easily.

Other proverbs on the theme of perseverance are CONSTANT DRIPPING WEARS AWAY THE STONE (90); IF AT FIRST YOU DON'T SUCCEED, TRY, TRY, TRY AGAIN (320); IT'S DOGGED THAT DOES IT (356); LITTLE BY LITTLE AND BIT BY BIT (415); LITTLE STROKES FELL GREAT OAKS (419); ROME WAS NOT BUILT IN A DAY (588); WHERE THERE'S A WILL THERE'S A WAY (755).

604   So many countries, so many customs

Every nationality has its own way of life and standard of behaviour.
See also WHEN IN ROME DO AS THE ROMANS DO (748).

605   A soft answer turneth away wrath

The source of this is Proverbs, xv, 1: 'A soft answer turneth away wrath; but grievous words stir up anger.' If anyone loses his temper and shouts at you, don't shout back. By answering him quietly and politely, you are much more likely to persuade him that he is being unjust and should not have lost his temper with you. As another proverb teaches us: IT TAKES TWO TO MAKE A QUARREL (374).

606   Some are wise and some are otherwise

This is a play on words. It means quite simply that some people are wise and others are not.

607 Some people cannot see the wood for the trees
When we stand in the middle of a wood, we can see only the trees immediately around us, but we know that the wood is there, for if there were no trees there would be no wood. People who, meta-phorically speaking, cannot see the wood for the trees are those who become so involved in detail that they cannot see the matter as a whole.

'Before we decide whether to have a public swimming pool,' said the Chairman of the Council, 'we must settle all the many minor questions that might arise.'

'Why not settle the main question first?' suggested a councillor. 'Do we or do we not want a swimming pool? With all respect, Mr Chairman, your trouble is that you can't see the wood for the trees.'

608 Sow the wind and reap the whirlwind
One evil leads to a worse.

The source is Hosea, viii, 7: 'For they have sown the wind, and they shall reap the whirlwind.'

609 Spare the rod and spoil the child
It does not improve a child's character if he is not punished when he has done wrong.

The source is Proverbs, xiii, 24: 'He that spareth his rod hateth his son: but he that loveth him chasteneth him betimes.' This appears in the Moffatt translation as: 'He hates his son who fails to ply the rod: the man who loves his son chastises him.'

610 Speak fair and think what you like
To 'speak fair' is to treat others with civility. Think what you like about them, but be polite when you speak to them. There is, however, the old saying: 'He that speaks me fair and loves me not, I'll treat him fair and trust him not.'

611 Speak the truth and shame the devil
Speak the truth boldly in defiance of strong temptation to tell lies.

612 Speak well of the dead
Speak well of them, for they cannot speak for themselves. 'Death softens all resentments,' wrote John Greenleaf Whittier, the American poet, 'and the consciousness of a common inheritance

of frailty and weakness modifies the severity of judgement.' The
Latin version is *De mortuis nil nisi bonum* – 'Of the dead nothing
but good.'

613 Speech is silver, silence is golden

Gold is more precious than silver, and there are times when it is
better to be silent than to speak.

Similar proverbs are HE CANNOT SPEAK WELL THAT CANNOT
HOLD HIS TONGUE (266); THERE IS A TIME TO SPEAK AND A TIME
TO BE SILENT (652).

614 The spirit is willing, but the flesh is weak

However willing we may be to do a thing, our physical condition
may prevent us from doing it.

The source is Matthew xxvi, 41. Here is the story as told in the
New English Bible:

Jesus then came with his disciples to a place called Gethsemane. He
said to them, 'Sit here while I go over there to pray.' He took with him
Peter and the two sons of Zebedee. Anguish and dismay came over him,
and he said to them, 'My heart is ready to break with grief. Stop here,
and stay awake with me.' He went on a little, fell on his face in prayer,
and said, 'My Father, if it is possible, let this cup pass me by. Yet not
as I will, but as thou wilt.'

He came to the disciples and found them asleep; and he said to Peter,
'What! Could none of you stay awake with me one hour? Stay awake,
and pray that you may be spared the test. The spirit is willing, but the
flesh is weak.'

615 Sticks and stones may break my bones, but words will never hurt me

However much one person insults another, he causes him no
physical injury at all. Only when words lead to blows are bones
liable to be broken.

The proverb, which dates back to the nineteenth century, was –
and still is – used mostly by children.

616 A still tongue makes a wise head

You will learn more by listening to other people than by talking
yourself.

617 Still waters run deep

'Shallow brooks murmur most, deep silent slide away,' wrote Sir

Philip Sidney. The fact that a man says little does not mean that he does not think profoundly, whilst those who talk the most have no depth of feeling. We find the same theme in such other proverbs as EMPTY VESSELS MAKE THE MOST SOUND (163).

618 The sting of a reproach is the truth of it
We can endure unjust reproaches, for we know that we do not deserve them. It is only when they are justified that they fill us with shame.

619 A stitch in time saves nine
By repairing a small tear now we avoid the necessity of repairing a large tear later on. In the same way, prompt action at an early stage may prevent serious trouble in the future. The proverb WHO REPAIRS NOT HIS GUTTERS REPAIRS HIS WHOLE HOUSE (763) teaches the folly of false economy and the effect of small things on greater ones. The man who repairs his gutters as soon as they show signs of needing attention can say as his reason for doing it: 'A stitch in time saves nine.'

A similar proverb is IT IS NO USE SPOILING THE SHIP FOR A HA'P'ORTH OF TAR (367).

620 Stolen pleasures are sweetest
This means the same as FORBIDDEN FRUIT IS SWEETEST (220). The things we most enjoy doing are those we know we ought not to be doing, such as watching cricket on the television when we should be working. If we had nothing else to do but watch cricket on the television we probably wouldn't enjoy it half so much!

621 A straw will show which way the wind blows
Small events can be a guide to momentous happenings. If the Foreign Secretary tells a taxi-driver at two o'clock in the morning to take him to the Prime Minister's residence and drive like the devil, we can suppose that an international crisis is looming.

See also COMING EVENTS CAST THEIR SHADOWS BEFORE (87).

622 The strength of the chain is in the weakest link
A chain is made up of a row of links fitted together. If all the links are strong, the chain will be strong also, but if even one link is

faulty, no greater strain can be put on the whole chain than can be put on that single weak link.

If a number of persons have joined together in some enterprise, the weakest link is he who lets down his companions by not playing his full part in the carrying out of their plans. For example, the conspiracy known as the Gunpowder Plot, the purpose of which was to blow up King James I and both Houses of Parliament on 5th November, 1605, the day fixed for the opening of parliament, failed because one of the plotters warned his brother-in-law not to attend the opening. Because of this weak link, the chain broke, and the Gunpowder Plot miscarried.

623   Stretch your legs according to your coverlet
This teaches adaptability. If when you lie full length your lower limbs are not covered by the bedclothes, you must bend your legs in order to keep warm. It also teaches prudence. If you stretch your legs beyond your coverlet, your feet will get cold. In other words, try always to adjust yourself to circumstances and live within your means.

See also CUT YOUR COAT ACCORDING TO YOUR CLOTH (102).

624   Strike while the iron is hot
Iron when it is red-hot is more easily bent and moulded than when it is cold. It should be struck before it has had time to cool down. Hence 'to strike while the iron is hot' is to choose the right moment to act, or to take advantage of a sudden opportunity.

'My boss,' said Amanda, 'is a rather bad-tempered man. Yesterday I caught him in a good humour for once and asked him for a day off. Was I surprised when he said yes!'

'Lucky you struck while the iron was hot,' laughed Trevor.

See also MAKE HAY WHILE THE SUN SHINES (436). Other proverbs on the theme of opportunity are listed under OPPORTUNITY SELDOM KNOCKS TWICE (546).

625   Submitting to one wrong brings on another
If you allow yourself to be victimized once, you will be victimized again.

626   Success has many friends
Those who have won big prizes in the pools will doubtless agree

with this! Another version is HE THAT HATH A FULL PURSE NEVER WANTED A FRIEND (275). From the social rather than the financial angle, a successful man gains the good opinions of those who had no time for him before he became famous. Whereas they snubbed him or ignored him then, now they seek his society.

627 Sufficient unto the day is the evil thereof
Don't add to the difficulties and problems of today by worrying about what is going to happen tomorrow.

The source is Matthew vi, 34 'Take therefore no thought for the morrow: for the morrow shall take thought for the things of itself. Sufficient unto the day is the evil thereof.'

Similar proverbs are DON'T CROSS A BRIDGE TILL YOU COME TO IT (125); DON'T CRY BEFORE YOU ARE HURT (126); DON'T MEET TROUBLE HALF-WAY (137); NEVER TROUBLE TROUBLE TILL TROUBLE TROUBLES YOU (496); TOMORROW IS ANOTHER DAY (691).

628 The sun is never the worse for shining on a dunghill
Good people are not corrupted by their surroundings.

629 Sweet are the uses of adversity
Misfortunes can sometimes be a blessing in disguise. In Shakespeare's *As You Like It*, the exiled duke in the forest of Arden finds he has much to be thankful for.

> Sweet are the uses of adversity,
> Which, like the toad, ugly and venomous,
> Wears yet a precious jewel in his head;
> And this our life exempt from public haunt
> Finds tongues in trees, books in the running brooks,
> Sermons in stones and good in everything.
> I would not change it.

T

630 The tailor makes the man
Good clothes can make a man look more impressive than he really is. The other proverb that comes immediately to mind is NEVER JUDGE BY APPEARANCES (487), yet it can also be said that a good tailor can help his customer to succeed in his career.

See also CLOTHES DO NOT MAKE THE MAN (86); FINE FEATHERS MAKE FINE BIRDS (206).

631   Take care of the pence and the pounds will take care of themselves
This teaches wise economy. Concentrate on saving small amounts and in time you will have a large amount.
Similar proverbs are EVERY LITTLE HELPS (179); MANY A LITTLE MAKES A MICKLE (446).

632   Take heed of the snake in the grass
Be on your guard against treachery.

633   Take not a musket to kill a butterfly
Don't take extreme measures to get rid of something quite trivial. Don't exaggerate your difficulties. We owe the following to an unknown poet:

> Don't make tragedies of trifles,
> Don't shoot butterflies with rifles—
>   Laugh it off!

A similar proverb is DON'T MAKE A MOUNTAIN OUT OF A MOLEHILL (134).

634   Take the bull by the horns
See THE BULL MUST BE TAKEN BY THE HORNS (62).

635   Take the rough with the smooth
Don't expect your road through life to be always easy. Accept bad times philosophically.

636   Take the will for the deed
Give a person credit for his good intentions, even though he does not act on them. He may have been anxious to help you, but circumstances have prevented him from doing so.

637   Take things as they come
Deal with things as they arise. DON'T CROSS A BRIDGE TILL YOU COME TO IT (125).

638 Take things as you find them
Adapt yourself to new surroundings or conditions. Another way
of saying this is WHEN IN ROME DO AS THE ROMANS DO (748).

639 Take time by the forelock
Seize the present moment. Old Father Time is represented as
being completely bald except for a lock of hair on his forehead.
You cannot catch him from behind but you can catch him from
the front by seizing him by the forelock. This proverb means that
time past cannot be used, but advantage can be taken of it *now*.
THERE IS NO TIME LIKE THE PRESENT (666) has the same meaning,
and a proverb with a similar meaning is A MILL CANNOT GRIND
WITH THE WATER THAT IS PAST (461).

640 A tale never loses in the telling
The facts of a story are usually improved upon in the telling. Lies
are condoned by Pooh-Bah in *The Mikado* as 'merely corrobora-
tive detail, intended to give artistic verisimilitude to a bald and
unconvincing narrative'. In *Henry IV, Part I* by Shakespeare, Sir
John Falstaff and three of his cronies are attacked by two other
cronies, Prince Henry and Poins, disguised as thieves. Falstaff's
party take to their heels. Back in the Boar's-Head Tavern in
Eastcheap, where they all meet later, Falstaff gives the Prince and
Poins a vivid account of the affair, in which they had fought with
and beaten off their attackers, the number of whom rises to fifty-
three before the tale is done. It has lost nothing in the telling!

641 Talk of the devil and he is sure to appear
We say this jokingly in shortened form when we are joined by a
person we have just been talking about.
    'Well, talk of the devil! Here *is* the old scoundrel! Is that right
you've got yourself engaged, Jack?'

642 Tastes differ
We all have our likes and dislikes. Similar proverbs are BEAUTY IS
IN THE EYE OF THE BEHOLDER (36); EVERYONE TO HIS TASTE (188);
ONE MAN'S MEAT IS ANOTHER MAN'S POISON (535); THERE IS NO
DISPUTING ABOUT TASTES (657).

643 Tell it not in Gath . . .
Don't spread scandal. Keep the story to yourself.

'Tell it not in Gath, but their marriage isn't turning out too well. There's good reason to believe . . .'

The source is II Samuel, i, 20. David said when he heard of the death of Jonathan in the war against the Philistines: 'Tell it not in Gath, publish it not in the streets of Askelon, lest the daughters of the Philistines rejoice.'

644 There are as good fish in the sea as ever came out of it
Just because you have lost one good opportunity, that does not mean that you will never get another. WHEN ONE DOOR SHUTS ANOTHER OPENS (749).

645 There are more ways of killing a cat than by choking it with cream
There is more than one way of achieving one's purpose.

646 There are tricks in every trade
Here 'tricks' are not crafty or deceitful acts, but ways of doing something successfully. To know the tricks of the trade is to have sound knowledge of the special skills needed for it. Loosely the saying refers to clever methods of attracting business or customers.

647 There are two sides to every question
In any argument or difference of opinion, neither side is entirely in the wrong. Much may be said on both sides.

648 There are wheels within wheels
In complex machinery the wheels that are apparently doing the work are turned by other, less obvious wheels. Figuratively, 'wheels within wheels' are indirect or secret agencies, out of sight, but in control of affairs.

'Why doesn't that fellow ever give a straight answer? He's the proprietor of the business – the one who should make the decisions – so why can't he say yes or no, there and then?'

'Because he's only a figure-head. The real boss works behind the scenes. Wheels within wheels, you know.'

649 There's a black sheep in every flock
This implies that there is a scoundrel in every family – a ne'er-do-well who is a disgrace to his parents and relatives.

650   There is a sin of omission as well as of commission
Here commission is performance, and omission is non-performance. You may be acting wrongly in doing a certain thing; you may be equally at fault in not doing a certain thing. For example, the sin of commission is drowning a person by pushing him into the canal; the sin of omission is making no attempt to rescue him when someone else has pushed him in. SILENCE GIVES CONSENT (601), so by keeping silent you have committed a sin of omission.

651   There is a tide in the affairs of men . . .
This comes in a speech by Brutus in Shakespeare's *Julius Caesar*:

> There is a tide in the affairs of men,
> Which, taken at the flood, leads on to fortune;
> Omitted, all the voyage of their life
> Is bound in shallows and in miseries.
> On such a full sea are we now afloat;
> And we must take the current when it serves,
> Or lose our ventures.

There is a right moment to undertake something successfully, and if we fail to grasp it, we do so at our peril.
Other proverbs on this theme are listed under OPPORTUNITY SELDOM KNOCKS TWICE (546).

652   There is a time to speak and a time to be silent
Sometimes it is prudent to say nothing, especially in consideration for other people's feelings. Similar proverbs are: HE CANNOT SPEAK WELL THAT CANNOT HOLD HIS TONGUE (266); SPEECH IS SILVER, SILENCE IS GOLDEN (613).

653   There is honour among thieves
A thief will not hesitate to steal from an honest man, but is reluctant to steal from another thief. A similar proverb is DOG DOES NOT EAT DOG (151).

654   There's many a good tune played on an old fiddle
A man's capabilities do not depend on his age.

655   There's many a slip 'twixt the cup and the lip
Dr Brewer recounts the story of Ancaeus, the helmsman of Jason's ship *Argo* in Greek mythology. 'He was told by a slave

that he would never live to taste the wine of his vineyards. When a bottle made from his own grapes was set before him, he sent for the slave to laugh at his prognostications; but the slave made answer, "There's many a slip 'twixt the cup and the lip." At this instant a messenger came in, and told Ancaeus that the Calydonian boar was laying his vineyard waste, whereupon he set down his cup, went out against the boar, and was killed in the encounter.'

Hence nothing is certain until you possess it.

Similar proverbs are CATCH YOUR BEAR BEFORE YOU SELL ITS SKIN (76); DON'T COUNT YOUR CHICKENS BEFORE THEY ARE HATCHED (124); DO NOT HALLOO TILL YOU ARE OUT OF THE WOOD (131); FIRST CATCH YOUR HARE (210); NEVER SPEND YOUR MONEY BEFORE YOU HAVE IT (493).

656   There's many a true word spoken in jest

Remarks not meant to be taken seriously frequently turn out to be true. For example:

'That's a nice car you've got there, Frank,' said his friend.

'Remember I said as a joke that I'd buy myself a new one if I won the pools? Well, this is it.'

'Congratulations! That proves there's many a true word spoken in jest.'

657   There is no disputing about tastes

No two people have the same likes and dislikes, or do things in the same way, so it is a waste of time to argue about it. Similar proverbs are BEAUTY IS IN THE EYE OF THE BEHOLDER (36); EVERYONE TO HIS TASTE (188); ONE MAN'S MEAT IS ANOTHER MAN'S POISON (535); TASTES DIFFER (642).

658   There's no fool like an old fool

This somewhat sweeping statement suggests that old fools are bigger fools than young ones. It is used as a comment on the actions of those we think should be sufficiently advanced in years to know better.

659   There is no garden without its weeds

Nothing is perfect. Even the best of us has his failings and weaknesses.

660   There is no peace for the wicked
We use this half-humorously when called upon to carry out some
unwelcome task.

'George,' said his wife, 'we want some more coal in from the
shed. The scuttle's empty.'

'There's no peace for the wicked,' he murmured, laying the
newspaper aside and rising to his feet.

The source is Isaiah, xlviii, 22: 'There is no peace, saith the Lord,
unto the wicked.'

661   There's no place like home
No matter how humble it may be, home is the place where one
feels happiest. The proverb comes from the famous song, *Home,
Sweet Home*, by John Howard Payne:

> 'Mid pleasures and palaces though we may roam,
> Be it ever so humble, there's no place like home!
> A charm from the skies seems to hallow us there,
> Which, seek through the world, ne'er is met with elsewhere.

A similar proverb is EAST OR WEST, HOME IS BEST (159).

662   There is no pleasure without pain
This may seem a sweeping statement, yet even the drunkard
doesn't achieve his pleasure without the pain of a hangover next
morning.

663   There is no rose without a thorn
A rose without a thorn is synonymous with impossible happiness.
However happy we are, there is always some little touch of sad-
ness or disappointment. Cynics may also apply this proverb to the
fair sex.

664   There is no royal road to learning
A royal road to anything is a way of attaining it without trouble
or effort, since a king's way (the royal road) is always made easy
for him. One cannot attain learning – that is, knowledge got by
study – without hard work.

See also A LITTLE LEARNING IS A DANGEROUS THING (417).

665   There is no smoke without fire
This refers to rumours, the argument being that all rumours are

based on fact; that although some may doubt the accuracy of a report that is passing from mouth to mouth, there must be some truth in it, however little.

'I hear Barglows are closing down their shop in West Street.'

'Surely not! They've got a fine business there.'

'Well, a number of people have told me that Barglows are feeling the pinch – and there's no smoke without fire.'

666 There is no time like the present

If a thing has to be done, do it now. Don't put it off till tomorrow. Remember that PROCRASTINATION IS THE THIEF OF TIME (567).

Similar proverbs are GATHER YE ROSEBUDS WHILE YE MAY (229); MAKE HAY WHILE THE SUN SHINES (436); NEVER PUT OFF TILL TOMORROW WHAT MAY BE DONE TODAY (491); ONE OF THESE DAYS IS NONE OF THESE DAYS (538); STRIKE WHILE THE IRON IS HOT (624); TAKE TIME BY THE FORELOCK (639); TOMORROW NEVER COMES (692); WHAT MAY BE DONE AT ANY TIME IS DONE AT NO TIME (735).

667 There is no wheat without chaff

Chaff is the outer covering of the grain and has to be separated from it. The proverb means that merit is often obscured by worthlessness. George Wither, the Jacobean poet, wrote this:

> Till from the straw the flail the corn doth beat,
> Until the chaff is purgèd from the wheat,
> Yea, till the mill the grains in pieces tear,
> The richness of the flour will scarce appear.

668 There is nothing new under the sun

The phrase 'under the sun' means 'in the world'. Even the very latest novelty is only something revived. As the French paradox has it: 'There is nothing new except that which has become antiquated.'

The source is Ecclesiastes, i, 9–10:

The thing that hath been, it is that which shall be; and that which is done is that which shall be done: and there is no new thing under the sun.

Is there any thing whereof it may be said, See, this is new? it hath been already of old time, which was before us.

669 · There is nothing permanent except change

This was the theory of Heraclitus, the Greek philosopher, who maintained that change is the only reality in nature.

670   There is nothing that costs less than civility
This means the same as COURTESY COSTS NOTHING (94).

671   There is safety in numbers
It is safer to be among the majority than among the minority; the more friends you have, the better it will be for you. The proverb is often applied to the man who avoids the danger of marriage by dividing his attentions among a number of girls.

672   They also serve who only stand and wait
This teaches patience. While others are actively concerned in some enterprise, there must be those who play a passive part, but without whom the enterprise may fail. Again, many people – firemen, for example – must remain idle at their posts until an emergency suddenly arises.

The proverb is the last line of Milton's sonnet on his blindness, which he feared would prevent him from writing and thereby serving God. He consoled himself with this thought:

> God does not need
> Either man's work, or His own gifts: who best
> Bear His mild yoke, they serve Him best: His state
> Is kingly; thousands at His bidding speed
> And post o'er land and ocean without rest:—
> They also serve who only stand and wait.

See also PATIENCE IS A VIRTUE (552).

673   They brag most who can do least
This has the same meaning as EMPTY VESSELS MAKE THE MOST SOUND (163).

674   The thin end of the wedge is dangerous
A wedge is a tool used to split logs of wood. The thick end is hammered and the thin end steadily widens the opening until the log falls apart. The proverb means that a small beginning will lead, it is hoped (or more often feared), to something greater.

'The building of just one house isn't going to spoil the beauty of this stretch of countryside.'

'But it's only the thin end of the wedge. One house will be followed by another, and before we know where we are there'll be scores of them.'

675 A thing of beauty is a joy for ever
This is the first line of *Endymion* by John Keats and extols the idea of beauty. However depressed we may be, 'Some shape of beauty moves away the pall from our dark spirits'. The beautiful object may perish but the joy of it lasts as long as the memory does.

676 A thing you don't want is dear at any price
If you don't want an article, however cheap it may be, it is dear because it is useless to you. This is a warning against the temptation to buy something just because it is cheap.

677 Things are seldom what they seem
As Buttercup and Captain Corcoran sing in *H.M.S. Pinafore*:

> Things are seldom what they seem,
> Skim milk masquerades as cream.

The moral is contained in another proverb, NEVER JUDGE BY APPEARANCES (487).

678 Things done cannot be undone
See WHAT'S DONE CANNOT BE UNDONE (729).

679 Think not on what you lack as much as on what you have
This teaches contentment. Count your blessings, not your wants.

680 Those who live in glass houses should not throw stones
The lesson this proverb teaches is that people whose own conduct is open to criticism should not criticize the conduct of others, who may retaliate by accusing their accusers.
    'When are you going to return that book I lent you over a month ago? It's downright dishonest to keep it so long.'
    'What about the one you borrowed from me early last year?'
    'I'm sorry. I'd forgotten all about that one.'
    'People who live in glass houses shouldn't throw stones.'

681 Those whom the gods love die young
This springs from a belief in an after-life that is better than this life. On this assumption a person who dies young is luckier than one who dies old. The gods love the young person so much that they cause him to die so as to have him with them earlier. This

idea was expressed in classical Greek as early as the third century B.C. and has survived because it is not inconsistent with Christianity.

682 Through hardship to the stars

Here 'stars' is synonymous with fame or renown. It is a translation of the Latin proverb, *Per aspera ad astra*, and means that the road to fame is rough and difficult. An alternative version, *Per ardua ad astra*, which means the same thing, is the motto of the Royal Air Force and is rarely used in its English translation.

A similar proverb is NO CROSS, NO CROWN (500).

683 Through obedience learn to command

This means the same as HE THAT CANNOT OBEY CANNOT COMMAND (271). See also IT NEEDS MORE SKILL THAN I CAN TELL TO PLAY THE SECOND FIDDLE WELL (371).

684 Throw out a sprat to catch a mackerel

If we use a small fish as a bait, we shall catch a larger one. It is worth sacrificing a little in order to gain a great deal more. A present to a rich aunt, given in the hope of inheriting her fortune, is a sprat to catch a mackerel.

A similar proverb is YOU MUST LOSE A FLY TO CATCH A TROUT (795).

685 Time and tide wait for no man

Do not delay taking action. If you wish to put to sea, do not miss the tide. Neither tide nor time will tarry for you. In a wider sense, if an opportunity presents itself, decide quickly and act promptly.

Other proverbs on this theme are listed under OPPORTUNITY SELDOM KNOCKS TWICE (546).

686 Time flies

This comes from the Latin, *Tempus fugit*. It means that time goes so quickly that it is difficult to keep pace with it.

687 Time is money

Time is as valuable as money. To waste time is as expensive as to waste money. Neither should be squandered.

688 Time is the great healer
However great our grief or disappointment may be, in the course
of time it will lessen. In this sense our 'wounds' heal with time.

689 Times change
What was true or valid at a time in the past is not necessarily so
today because circumstances change. The proverb encourages us
to keep up to date and adapt our views to changed conditions.
ONE CANNOT PUT BACK THE CLOCK (529).

690 To err is human
We are all liable to make mistakes. The saying dates back to
classical times. We find it, for instance, in Seneca: 'Humanum est
errare'. Alexander Pope used it in his *Essay on Criticism* (1711):

> Good nature and good sense must ever join;
> To err is human, to forgive, divine.

Similar proverbs are EVEN HOMER SOMETIMES NODS (169); NO
MAN IS INFALLIBLE (506).

691 Tomorrow is another day
We should not behave as if this were the last day. There is always
another day tomorrow, and always the hope that things will get
better. SUFFICIENT UNTO THE DAY IS THE EVIL THEREOF (627).

692 Tomorrow never comes
'I'll do it tomorrow,' Tom promised his mother.
'Tomorrow never comes,' she said. 'Do it now.'
Tomorrow is always the day after today. If today is Thursday
it will be yesterday tomorrow, and Friday will be today. The
saying is used as a warning that PROCRASTINATION IS THE THIEF
OF TIME (567).

693 The tongue ever turns to the aching tooth
Similarly do our thoughts keep on coming back to something that
is worrying us

694 The tongue is not steel, yet it cuts
A sharp tongue wounds. If you do not wish to hurt people's
feelings, do not speak too harshly. As it says in the Apocrypha:

'Many have fallen by the edge of the sword: but not so many as have fallen by the tongue.'

A similar proverb is THE PEN IS MIGHTIER THAN THE SWORD (553).

695 Too many cooks spoil the broth
Although MANY HANDS MAKE LIGHT WORK (447), there should be only one cook in a kitchen. If there are several of them they will disagree with each other, get in each other's way, put too much salt in this and too much pepper in that, and spoil not only the soup but probably the whole meal also.

The same thing applies to most other enterprises. If too many people try to do the same thing at the same time, chaos will reign.

696 Too much curiosity lost Paradise
It doesn't do to be too curious or inquisitive. The proverb is a quotation from *The Lucky Chance*, a play by Aphra Behn. The reference is, of course, to the story of Adam and Eve, who were expelled from the garden of Eden because they had tasted the forbidden fruit (see FORBIDDEN FRUIT IS SWEETEST (220)).

Similar proverbs are EAVESDROPPERS NEVER HEAR ANY GOOD OF THEMSELVES (161); THE FISH WILL SOON BE CAUGHT THAT NIBBLES AT EVERY BAIT (214); HE WHO PEEPS THROUGH A HOLE MAY SEE WHAT WILL VEX HIM. (294)

697 A tree is known by its fruit
Men are judged by what they do.

The sources are Matthew, xii, 33 and Luke, vi, 44. Here is the second of these as given in the New English Bible:

> There is no such thing as a good tree producing worthless fruit, nor yet a worthless tree producing good fruit. For each tree is known by its own fruit: you do not gather figs from thistles, and you do not pick grapes from brambles. A good man produces good from the store of good within himself; and an evil man from evil within produces evil.

698 Truth is stranger than fiction
More curious things happen in real life than have ever been invented by writers of sensational stories. We often use the saying when we hear of some remarkable occurrence.

699 The truth will out

Truth cannot be concealed indefinitely. A similar proverb is
MURDER WILL OUT (477). As Shakespeare makes a character say
in *The Merchant of Venice*: 'Truth will come to light; murder
cannot be hid long.'

700 Two blacks do not make a white

Your faults are not excused by the faults of somebody else.

'Jack often travels on the train without a ticket, so why shouldn't I?'

'Just because he does it, that's no reason why you should. Two
blacks don't make a white.'

A proverb with the same meaning is TWO WRONGS DO NOT
MAKE A RIGHT (705).

701 Two dogs fight for a bone, and a third runs away with it

While two persons are disputing over something, somebody else
takes advantage of the fact that their attention is distracted. For
example, there was only one vacant seat left in the crowded hall.
Mr Smith and Mr Brown were arguing about which of them had
the prior right to it, when Mr Robinson stepped past them and
sat down in it.

702 Two heads are better than one

It is an advantage to confer with somebody else before reaching
an important decision.

'I've got a problem on my mind, Harry. Give me the benefit of
your advice, will you? Two heads are better than one.'

'As long as you don't mean "Two fools are better than one"!'

703 Two is company, three is none

This is sometimes quoted as 'Two's company, three's a crowd'.
Two friends often agree well on their own; but the presence of a
third may lead to quarrelling. The saying can express the senti-
ments of courting couples in particular.

704 Two of a trade can never agree

They are both too envious, each imagining that the other is
cleverer or better off than he.

705 Two wrongs do not make a right

This means the same as TWO BLACKS DO NOT MAKE A WHITE (700).

U

706   Uneasy lies the head that wears a crown
This is the penalty of greatness.

> None are completely wretched but the great,
> Superior woes superior stations bring;
> A peasant sleeps, while cares awake a king.

Thus wrote William Broome, the eighteenth-century clergyman
and poet. This is an echo of Shakespeare's *Henry IV*, Part II.
'Uneasy lies the head that wears a crown' is the last line of the
speech by the King beginning: 'How many thousand of my poorest
subjects are at this hour asleep!'

707   United we stand, divided we fall
Unity is strength. As long as we stick together we shall be safe.
If we begin to quarrel among ourselves, our opponents will
strike us down one by one.
  Similar proverbs are A HOUSE DIVIDED AGAINST ITSELF CANNOT
STAND (314); THERE IS SAFETY IN NUMBERS (671).

V

708   Variety is the spice of life
Life becomes very monotonous without some break in the daily
routine. William Cowper wrote in his long poem, *The Task*:

> Variety is the very spice of life,
> That gives it all its flavour.

A somewhat similar proverb is ALL WORK AND NO PLAY
MAKES JACK A DULL BOY (17).

709   Verb. sap.
This, in its abbreviated form, is one of those proverbs that have
remained more common in the original than in the English translation. It is the Latin for A WORD IS ENOUGH TO THE WISE (770).

710   Virtue is its own reward
The reward for behaving virtuously is the satisfaction one feels in

doing what one knows to be right. The proverb is often used to warn that we should not expect material rewards for acting virtuously.

711 The voice of the people is the voice of God
This comes to us from the Latin: *Vox populi vox Dei.* Dr Brewer made these comments: 'This does not mean that the voice of the many is wise and good, but only that it is irresistible. You might as well try to stop the tide of the Atlantic as to resist the *vox populi.*'

W

712 Wake not a sleeping lion
Don't ask for trouble. It's safer to leave things as they are. A similar proverb is LET SLEEPING DOGS LIE (397).

713 Walls have ears
Be careful what you say and where you say it. There may be someone lurking on the other side of the wall, or, to bring the proverb up to date, there may be a hidden microphone *in* the wall.

714 Want is the mother of industry
Dire need forces people to work, to make enough money to live. See also NECESSITY IS THE MOTHER OF INVENTION (480).

715 Waste not, want not
If you are economical and careful with your money, you need never want – that is, be without the necessities of life.
A similar proverb is KEEP SOMETHING FOR A RAINY DAY (379).

716 A watched pot never boils
When we are looking forward to something, time always seems to pass very slowly, just as it does when we are standing impatiently waiting for the kettle to come to the boil.
'This is awful!' said Mary. 'Jack promised to phone me this evening and the bell just *won't* ring. If I have to wait much longer I shall scream!'

'If I were you, dear,' her mother advised, 'I should get on with something else. As dear old Granny used to say, a watched pot never boils.'

717   Water is a boon in the desert, but the drowning man curses it
In this life we either have too little of what we do want, or too much of what we don't want or can't use. The same thought is to be found in THE GODS SEND NUTS TO THOSE WHO HAVE NO TEETH (243).

See also CIRCUMSTANCES ALTER CASES (84).

718   The way to a man's heart is through his stomach
This is good advice for wives. Keep your husband well fed and he will always love you.

719   We are all slaves of opinion
Here 'opinion' is 'public opinion'. Our actions are influenced by what other people may say or think about them. WHAT WILL MRS GRUNDY SAY? (740).

720   We soon believe what we desire
We soon believe what we want to believe. See THE WISH IS FATHER TO THE THOUGHT (768).

721   The weakest goes to the wall
To 'go to the wall' is to be thrust aside. In the battle for survival it is the weak who suffer most.

722   Wedlock is a padlock
This is a play on words. Wedlock is the married state, in which you are imprisoned as if by a padlock. There is no escape! See HE TRAVELS THE FASTEST WHO TRAVELS ALONE (284); MARRY IN HASTE, AND REPENT AT LEISURE (452).

723   Well begun is half done
If you start a thing badly it takes a long time to finish it, because the bad start seriously affects the later work. But if you make a good start, everything follows naturally and easily. For example if the foundations of a house are sound and well constructed, the house is better built and put up more rapidly than if it has to be erected on faulty foundations.

724   What can you expect from a hog but a grunt?
This is a rhetorical question needing no reply. It means something
on the lines of: 'Why are you surprised by his rude behaviour?
It's all you can expect from such a pig of a man.'
    See also YOU CANNOT MAKE A SILK PURSE OUT OF A SOW'S EAR
(784).

725   What can't be cured must be endured
If nothing can be done to improve the situation, we must put up
with it. The proverb can be used as a retort to somebody who
complains about the weather or the Government or noisy motor-
cycles or whatever it is he particularly objects to.
    A similar proverb is YOU MUST GRIN AND BEAR IT (794).

726   What costs little is little esteemed
We tend to value things by the amount we pay for them, which is
not always their true worth. The same article may cost twice as
much in the fashionable store as it does in the little shop round
the corner, yet we try to keep up with the Joneses by buying it at
the store.
    The same applies to other things. For example, good health
costs nothing, yet we do not value it until we have ceased to enjoy
it.

727   What is a workman without his tools?
The cleverest of craftsmen cannot make things with his bare
hands. Similarly, if we are to undertake a task we must have the
means of doing it.
    See GIVE US THE TOOLS, AND WE WILL FINISH THE JOB (237).
See also YOU CANNOT MAKE BRICKS WITHOUT STRAW (786).

728   What is bred in the bone will never come out of the flesh
This saying is often misquoted and misconstrued. People say,
'What's bred in the bone will come out in the flesh', meaning that
a natural tendency cannot be restrained (e.g. Once a liar, always
a liar). This is incorrect. The real meaning is to do with heredity:
we inherit certain characteristics from our ancestors, and those
same characteristics will be inherited from us by our descendants.
Once it is 'in the flesh' it will never come out.
    See also LIKE FATHER, LIKE SON (409).

729   What's done cannot be undone
It is too late to regret an action after it has been performed. IT IS
NO USE CRYING OVER SPILT MILK (366).
See also A WORD SPOKEN IS PAST RECALLING (771).

730   What is sauce for the goose is sauce for the gander
Whether we eat goose or gander, we have the same apple sauce
with it, so what is good for one is good for the other. If Barry plays
a practical joke on George, then complains when George does
the same thing to him, George can say: 'What's sauce for the
goose is sauce for the gander. Fair's fair.'

731   What is the good of a sundial in the shade?
A sundial tells the time only when the sun is shining upon it. If it
is placed where the sun cannot reach it, it will never tell the time.
The moral is that talents should not be hidden.

> Hide not your talents, they for use were made.
> What's a Sun-dial in the Shade?
>
> (Benjamin Franklin)

See also HIDE NOT YOUR LIGHT UNDER A BUSHEL (304).

732   What is worth doing is worth doing well
This is treated under IF A THING IS WORTH DOING IT IS WORTH
DOING WELL (319).

733   What's yours is mine, and what's mine is my own
This is a skit on the quotation from Shakespeare's *Measure for
Measure*: 'What's mine is yours, and what is yours is mine.' A
similar saying is: 'Heads I win, tails you lose.'

734   What man has done, man can do
Once a thing has been done, however difficult or dangerous it may
be, it can be done again. Take, for example, the exploration of
space. On 12th April, 1961, Major Gagarin of the U.S.S.R. circled
the earth in Vostok I; on 5th May of the same year Commander
Shepherd of the U.S.A. attained a height of 117 miles in a space
capsule; and on 6th August Major Titov made seventeen orbits
of the earth in Vostok II.

735   What may be done at any time is done at no time
This is another way of saying ONE OF THESE DAYS IS NONE OF
THESE DAYS (538). 'I'll do it one of these days.' This means that
you propose to do whatever it is later on. The result is that it is
never done at all.

736   What must be must be
We have no alternative but to bow to the inevitable. It is a philo-
sophical acceptance of things as they are.
   Similar proverbs are DO NOT KICK AGAINST THE PRICKS (133);
WHAT CAN'T BE CURED MUST BE ENDURED (725); YOU MUST
GRIN AND BEAR IT (794).

737   What one loses on the swings one makes up on the roundabouts
The proprietor of a fair ground does not mind running his swings
at a loss if his roundabouts bring him in a handsome profit. He
can afford to provide swings for the few people who enjoy them
and who will very likely pay to go on the roundabouts as well.
Similarly a newsagent may make a much smaller profit on newspapers than on other goods he sells, yet finds newspapers good for
trade because customers who call in for them will often buy other
things at the same time.
   Another aspect of the proverb is that although the swings make
less profit than the roundabouts today, they may make more profit
than the roundabouts tomorrow.

738   What soberness conceals, drunkenness reveals
A sober man keeps a guard on his tongue, holding back anything
he wishes to hide. Strong drink unseals his lips and he tells everything.
   A similar proverb is IN WINE THERE IS TRUTH (346), the Latin
version of which is *In vino veritas* (345).

739   What the eye doesn't see the heart doesn't grieve over
We are not worried by things that go on without our knowledge.
For example, if the chef in a restaurant makes a practice of
spitting in the frying-pan to make sure the temperature is right
for the *Crêpes Suzette*, the diners are not distressed, since they do
not see it happen.
   A similar proverb is WHERE IGNORANCE IS BLISS, 'TIS FOLLY
TO BE WISE (754).

740 What will Mrs Grundy say?
What will the neighbours say? As is mentioned under WE ARE ALL
SLAVES OF OPINION (719), our actions are influenced by what other
people may say or think about them. In a play called *Speed the
Plough* by Thomas Morton and first produced in 1798, Mrs
Grundy is the symbol of conventional propriety. She does not
appear in the play, but her neighbour, Dame Ashfield, is con-
stantly afraid of incurring her disapproval.

741 Whatsoever a man soweth, that shall he also reap
See AS YOU SOW, SO SHALL YOU REAP (24).

742 When all men speak, no man hears
Unless we listen to each other, we shall learn nothing.

743 When children stand quiet they have done some ill
The rhymed version of this is:

> When children stand still,
> They have done some ill.

A mother once said to her daughter: 'Tommy's very quiet. Go
and find out what he's doing, dear, and tell him he mustn't.'

744 When Greek meets Greek, then comes the tug of war
When two adversaries are of equal strength of character, the
contest of wills is certain to be long and hard-fought.
    Dr Brewer tells us that the reference is to the obstinate resis-
tance of the Greek cities to Philip and his son Alexander, the
Macedonian kings, who were also Greeks by descent.
    The proverb as given above has become so established that we
cannot change it now, yet it is a misquotation. The correct version,
in a play called *The Rival Queens* by Nathaniel Lee, is: 'When
Greeks join'd Greeks, then was the tug of war.' The verb 'to join'
means here 'to fight' and a tug is a decisive contest. The athletic
event derives its name from this.
    It should be noted that when we use the proverb we are not
referring to battles long ago, but to a difference of opinion between two strong-minded men.
    A similar proverb is DIAMOND CUT DIAMOND (115).

745 When I lent I had a friend; when I asked he was unkind
This means the same as LEND YOUR MONEY AND LOSE YOUR

FRIEND (391). See also NEITHER A BORROWER NOR A LENDER BE (483).

746 When in doubt do nowt
This is an old Cheshire proverb, 'nowt' meaning 'nothing'. It is better to refrain from action than to do something you are not sure about. There is much to be said for what Sir James Mackintosh once described as 'a wise and masterly inactivity'.

747 When in doubt leave out
This advice applies particularly to writers who are either not sure of their facts, or cannot make up their minds whether or not to include a passage that pleases them but may not please all their readers.
  'Dear Arthur – Many thanks for letting me read the manuscript of your reminiscences. I find them lively and interesting reading, but venture to suggest leaving out the anecdote about the noble Lord, the Admiral's daughter and the cauliflowers. It's certainly very funny, but you don't want a libel action on your hands.'

748 When in Rome do as the Romans do
If you are away from home, adapt yourself to your surroundings and to the local customs. Don't expect the people there to alter their way of life just to please you. Lord Chesterfield wrote to his son on 2nd October 1747: 'Good-breeding, as it is called, is different in almost every country, and merely local; and every man of sense imitates and conforms to that local good-breeding of the place he is at.'

749 When one door shuts another opens
Failure should not deter us, for there are always other opportunities.
  A similar proverb is THERE ARE AS GOOD FISH IN THE SEA AS EVER CAME OUT OF IT (644).

750 When the cat is away the mice will play
This is a very old proverb, dating back to the sixteenth century. It means that when the person in authority is away, those under him will take advantage of his absence.

'We had a simply marvellous time at school today. Miss Gowland was in bed with 'flu, and poor little Mrs Williamson can't keep order for nuts!'

751 When the wolf comes in at the door, love creeps out of the window
The 'wolf' is poverty. When a young couple marry without enough money to keep them in a manner to which they have become accustomed, this is called 'love in a cottage'. The love lasts as long as the money, but not a day longer, so the proverb says.
See also FIRST THRIVE AND THEN WIVE (213).

752 When the word is out it belongs to another
Once we have said it, we cannot get it back. This proverb has the same meaning as A WORD SPOKEN IS PAST RECALLING (771).
See also WHAT'S DONE CANNOT BE UNDONE (729).

753 When thieves fall out, honest men come by their own
If thieves are squabbling among themselves, they are too busy to rob honest men. The phrase 'come by their own' means 'keep what belongs to them'.

754 Where ignorance is bliss, 'tis folly to be wise
If knowledge brings unhappiness it is better to be ignorant.
The proverb comes from Thomas Gray's *Ode on a Distant Prospect of Eton College*. The poet sadly considers the future of the boys there:

> Alas! regardless of their doom
>   The little victims play!
> No sense have they of ills to come
>   Nor care beyond the day.

The last six lines of the poem run:

> Yet, ah! why should they know their fate,
> Since sorrow never comes too late,
> And happiness too swiftly flies?
> Thought would destroy their paradise!
> No more; – where ignorance is bliss,
>   'Tis folly to be wise.

A similar proverb is WHAT THE EYE DOESN'T SEE THE HEART DOESN'T GRIEVE OVER (739).

755   Where there's a will there's a way

Given sufficient determination, we can accomplish what we set out to do.

Other proverbs on this theme are CONSTANT DRIPPING WEARS AWAY THE STONE (90); IF AT FIRST YOU DON'T SUCCEED, TRY, TRY, TRY AGAIN (320); IT'S DOGGED THAT DOES IT (356); LITTLE BY LITTLE AND BIT BY BIT (415); LITTLE STROKES FELL GREAT OAKS (419); ROME WAS NOT BUILT IN A DAY (588); SLOW BUT SURE WINS THE RACE (603).

756   Where there's muck there's brass

You can earn good money if you don't mind dirtying your hands.

Another version of this proverb is MUCK AND MONEY GO TOGETHER (476); 'brass' is a slang word for money. We can appreciate the point of these sayings when we find ourselves in a great industrial area, with its factories and foundries, its smoky atmosphere, its coal mines, its ironstone mines, its clay mines, its slagheaps.

In one of its senses 'muck' is the material removed in the process of mining. It has to be separated from the ores, and its presence in great pyramids shows that much valuable stuff has been extracted as well.

Both sayings can apply also to a craftsman – a potter, perhaps – who has not the time to clear up the mess behind him because he is too busy turning out marketable products.

757   Where there is smoke there is fire

See THERE IS NO SMOKE WITHOUT FIRE (665).

758   Whether the pitcher strikes the stone, or the stone the pitcher, it is bad for the pitcher

Whichever side starts the fight, the weaker side will get the worst of it.

759   While there is life there is hope

The outlook may be grim and the future dark, yet while we still have life within us there is always the possibility that the situation will improve. We may win the pools!

Similar proverbs are EVERY CLOUD HAS A SILVER LINING (171); HOPE SPRINGS ETERNAL IN THE HUMAN BREAST (313); NEVER SAY DIE (492); NOTHING SO BAD BUT MIGHT HAVE BEEN WORSE (520).

760 Who chatters to you will chatter of you
Whoever tells you tales about other people will tell other people tales about *you*.

761 Who is worse shod than the shoemaker's wife?
The shoemaker is so anxious to make every penny he can out of his trade that he even denies his wife a new pair of shoes. Some other husbands tend to be equally selfish.

762 Who keeps company with the wolf will learn to howl
This means that if you mix with evil companions you will soon be as wicked as they are. Similar proverbs are HE SHOULD HAVE A LONG SPOON THAT SUPS WITH THE DEVIL (270); HE THAT TOUCHETH PITCH SHALL BE DEFILED (279); THE ROTTEN APPLE INJURES ITS NEIGHBOURS (590).

763 Who repairs not his gutters repairs his whole house
This teaches the folly of false economy and the effect of small things on greater ones. By not spending the small amount needed to repair the gutters, the owner of the house is liable to pay a much larger sum later on for putting right the damage caused to the house by water leaking from the gutters.
Similar proverbs are IT IS NO USE SPOILING THE SHIP FOR A HA'P'ORTH OF TAR (367); A STITCH IN TIME SAVES NINE (619).

764 Why keep a dog and bark yourself?
Householders keep dogs to guard their homes by barking when they hear suspicious sounds outside. Figuratively, 'to keep a dog and bark yourself' is to do the work that you pay others to do for you.
'Isn't it about time you clipped the front hedge, Henry?' asked his wife.
'That's the gardener's job,' he answered. 'Why should I keep a dog and bark myself?'

765 Win at first and lose at last
This is a saying among card-players. Those who win in the early stages of the game usually finish up as losers.

766 A wise man is never less alone than when alone
Wise people are resourceful and do not feel the lack of company

when alone, because they can find plenty to do and plenty to think about.

767 Wise men learn by other men's mistakes; fools by their own
It is better to keep out of trouble by not repeating the foolish behaviour of others than it is to do as they did and suffer in the same way.

A similar proverb is EXPERIENCE IS THE TEACHER OF FOOLS (197).

768 The wish is father to the thought
We soon believe what we want to believe. In World War II we called it 'wishful thinking', which is defined in *The Shorter Oxford English Dictionary* as 'an illusory state of mind towards events which is coloured by one's wishes concerning the future, especially as to what one hopes will happen'.

The proverb can be traced back to Latin and appears in a slightly different form in Shakespeare's *Henry IV*, Part II, when Prince Henry says to his dying father: 'I never thought to hear you speak again.' To this the King replies:

> Thy wish was father, Harry, to that thought:
> I stay too long for thee, I weary thee.
> Dost thou so hunger for mine empty chair
> That thou wilt needs invest thee with my honours
> Before thy hour be ripe? O foolish youth!

His Majesty is not so far gone that he cannot deliver forty-one lines of rebuke before Prince Hal gets a chance to explain himself.

769 A wonder lasts but nine days
A nine days' wonder is an event that attracts much attention, but is soon forgotten. Dr Brewer divides the nine days into 'three days' amazement, three days' discussion of details, and three days' subsidence' – that is, sinking down.

770 A word is enough to the wise
An intelligent person can readily take a hint. Whoever is speaking to him knows that he does not need a long explanation. The Latin version is *verbum sat sapienti*, but we usually omit *sat* (enough) and abbreviate the rest to *verb. sap.* in such contexts as:

'Verb. sap.,' he said when she tried to explain. 'I can guess the rest.'

A somewhat similar proverb is A NOD IS AS GOOD AS A WINK (510).

771   A word spoken is past recalling

Once you have said a thing, it is too late to regret having said it. We find the following in *The Rubáiyát of Omar Khayyám*, translated by Edward FitzGerald:

> The Moving Finger writes; and, having writ,
> Moves on: nor all thy Piety nor Wit
>   Shall lure it back to cancel half a Line,
> Nor all thy Tears wash out a Word of it.

See also WHAT'S DONE CANNOT BE UNDONE (729).

772   Words cut more than swords

This means the same as THE TONGUE IS NOT STEEL, YET IT CUTS (694).

773   The worse luck now, the better another time

Just as we are not always lucky, so we are not always unlucky. The colloquial phrase is: 'Better luck next time.' A similar proverb is EVERY DOG HAS HIS DAY (173).

774   Worse things happen at sea

We say this in a resigned tone when we find ourselves in an awkward or difficult situation, or when we have to put up with something less than we expected.

'The butcher hasn't delivered the joint,' said Mrs Jones, 'so I'll have to open a tin of something.'

'Never mind,' said her husband. 'Worse things happen at sea.'

775   The worst wheel of the cart creaks most

The inefficient or lazy worker is the one who does all the complaining.

776   The worth of a thing is best known by the want of it

It is only when we have been deprived of something that we appreciate the true value of it. One illustration of this is, of course, the other proverb: ABSENCE MAKES THE HEART GROW FONDER (1).

Y

777 You cannot burn the candle at both ends

Dr Brewer explains this as follows: 'You cannot do two opposite things at one and the same time; you cannot exhaust your energies in one direction, and yet reserve them unimpaired for something else. If you go to bed late you cannot get up early.'

'I've got to get this ironing done,' said Mrs Mills.

'But it's after midnight,' protested her husband. 'Far better come to bed, and do the ironing in the morning. Burning the candle at both ends isn't good for you.'

Other proverbs on the theme of 'either – or' are A DOOR MUST BE EITHER SHUT OR OPEN (152); NO MAN CAN SERVE TWO MASTERS (502); YOU CANNOT HAVE IT BOTH WAYS (781); YOU CANNOT HAVE YOUR CAKE AND EAT IT (782); YOU CANNOT RUN WITH THE HARE AND HUNT WITH THE HOUNDS (788); YOU CANNOT SELL THE COW AND DRINK THE MILK (789); YOU CANNOT SERVE GOD AND MAMMON (790).

778 You cannot catch old birds with chaff

Experienced people are not to be deceived; they are too shrewd. Chaff is the outer covering of the grain and worthless as food.

779 You cannot get a quart into a pint pot

This incontestable fact is used figuratively in such contexts as:

'Look, dear,' said Mr Davison while his wife was packing for their summer holidays, 'ours is a car, not a motor-coach. You can't get a quart into a pint pot, so we'll have to make do with much less luggage.'

780 You cannot get blood out of a stone

Here 'blood' means human feeling and a 'stone' represents a hard-hearted person. The proverb refers to avarice; a man can be so full of greed and lust for wealth that he feels no sympathy at all for others. To ask his help is as useless as trying to get blood out of a stone. An alternative is YOU CANNOT GET WATER OUT OF A STONE, which has more the meaning of the futility of trying to extract money from a person who either will not pay, or has not the money to pay with.

781   You cannot have it both ways
You may not choose first one and then the other alternative in order to suit your own convenience. It is often used in argument when an opponent shifts his ground.

Other proverbs on the theme of 'either – or' are listed under YOU CANNOT BURN THE CANDLE AT BOTH ENDS (777).

782   You cannot have your cake and eat it
This is sometimes given as: 'You cannot eat your cake and have it.' They both mean the same thing, which is that if a choice has to be made between alternatives, you must have one or the other, not both. Again, you can't spend your money and save it at the same time.

Other proverbs on the theme of 'either – or' are listed under YOU CANNOT BURN THE CANDLE AT BOTH ENDS (777).

783   You cannot make a crab walk straight
This warns us never to attempt the impossible. You can no more make a crab walk any way but sideways than you can change a person's character.

784   You cannot make a silk purse out of a sow's ear
Dr Brewer had this to say: 'You must have the necessary materials or facilities before you can make or do what you are expected to … A sow's ear may somewhat resemble a purse, but it cannot be made into a purse.' By extension this means that you cannot change a person's real character. All the education in the world will not turn a vulgar, low-minded ruffian into a gentleman, or a slattern into a lady.

A similar proverb is WHAT CAN YOU EXPECT FROM A HOG BUT A GRUNT? (724).

785   You cannot make an omelet without breaking eggs
You cannot expect to get something for nothing. You must be prepared to make sacrifices in order to gain your ends.

'We shall be much more comfortable in our new house, but I'm afraid it's not going to be so cheap to run as this one.'

'You can't make an omelet without breaking eggs.'

786   You cannot make bricks without straw
Nothing can be made without the necessary materials.

'The trouble is,' said the captain of the Cricket Club at a meeting of the committee, 'that young chaps today aren't interested in the game, so there's no chance of running a second eleven. You can't make bricks without straw.'

In Biblical times bricks were made of mud and straw dried in the sun, the straw holding the mud together. The source of the proverb is to be found in the fifth chapter of Exodus.

A similar proverb is WHAT IS A WORKMAN WITHOUT HIS TOOLS? (727).

787   You cannot put old heads on young shoulders

You cannot expect young people to be as wise and prudent as their elders.

788   You cannot run with the hare and hunt with the hounds

Figuratively, 'running with the hare and hunting with the hounds' is the deceitful behaviour of one who fights on one side and gives secret help to the other side. Terms for these traitors to the cause are 'double-dealers' and 'double-crossers'. A very old saying, dating back to the fifteenth century, is: 'Thou hast a crooked tongue, holding with the hound and running with the hare.' Invariably these tricksters are found out; they should be loyal to one side or the other.

Other proverbs on the theme of 'either – or' are listed under YOU CANNOT BURN THE CANDLE AT BOTH ENDS (777).

789   You cannot sell the cow and drink the milk

You cannot enjoy the milk and have at the same time the advantage of the money got for the cow. In other words, you must have one thing or the other, not both.

Other proverbs on the theme of 'either – or' are listed under YOU CANNOT BURN THE CANDLE AT BOTH ENDS (777).

790   You cannot serve God and mammon

Mammon is the god of riches. You must choose between godliness and worldliness. The source is Matthew vi, 24, which is quoted under NO MAN CAN SERVE TWO MASTERS (502).

Other proverbs on the theme of 'either – or' are listed under YOU CANNOT BURN THE CANDLE AT BOTH ENDS (777).

791 You cannot teach an old dog new tricks
As people get older they grow more set in their ways and do not welcome any innovation.

792 You may know by a handful the whole sack
The quality of the contents of a sack of corn, flour, etc. may be judged by the quality of a sample. Putting it another way, we do not have to eat the whole egg to know that it is bad.

The proverb means that we can judge a person's character on very small evidence. For example, a generous action suggests a kindly nature, and a callous remark a hard, unfeeling heart.

793 You may lead a horse to the water, but you cannot make him drink
You may be acting in the best interests of the horse by taking him to the trough, but if he doesn't want to drink he's not going to – and that's that. Similarly, you can do your utmost to make a person share your views, yet there is a point beyond which he will not go.

'I've listened to your arguments with the closest attention, Professor, and I have read carefully all the books you recommended, but I still can't agree with you.'

794 You must grin and bear it
This does not necessarily mean that you should endure misfortunes or difficulties with a broad smile, but rather that you should put up with them philosophically.

'My wife has just flown out to Canada to stay with her sister for a month. I'm not looking forward to having the kids on my hands and trying to keep the home going while she's away, but I'll have to grin and bear it.'

See also WHAT CAN'T BE CURED MUST BE ENDURED (725).

795 You must lose a fly to catch a trout
The fly is the bait on the angler's hook. This proverb means the same as THROW OUT A SPRAT TO CATCH A MACKEREL (684). It is worth sacrificing a little in order to gain a great deal more.

796 You never know what you can do till you try
Don't be a faint-heart and say, 'I'll never manage to do it.' Have a go, and you'll be surprised at your own ability.

797   You scratch my back and I'll scratch yours

You praise me and I'll praise you; you flatter me and I'll flatter you. Such a reciprocal arrangement has been described as a Mutual Admiration Society with a membership of two.

798   The young will sow their wild oats

To sow one's wild oats is to commit youthful excesses or follies and, having committed them, to mend one's ways. Thomas Nashe wrote over four hundred years ago:

> Youth ne'er aspires to virtues perfect grown
> Till his wild oats be sown.

799   Youth will be served

Another version is YOUTH WILL HAVE ITS COURSE. Let the young enjoy themselves while they can.

> When all the world is young, lad,
>   And all the trees are green;
> And every goose a swan, lad,
>   And every lass a queen;
> Then hey, for boot and horse, lad,
>   And round the world away;
> Young blood must have its course, lad,
>   And every dog his day.
>
> (Charles Kingsley)

Z

800   Zeal without knowledge is a runaway horse

Zeal is defined in *The Concise Oxford Dictionary* as 'earnestness or fervour in advancing a cause or rendering service; hearty and persistent endeavour'. But zeal must go hand in hand with experience. The enthusiasm of an inexperienced person may do more harm than good.

Biographical Details concerning those mentioned in this book

ARISTOTLE (384–322 B.C.), Greek philosopher.

BACON, Francis (1561–1626), English philosopher and statesman.

BEHN, Aphra (1840–89), English dramatist and novelist, the first woman professional writer.

BENNETT, Enoch Arnold (1867–1931), English writer.

BORROW, George Henry (1803–81), English author.

BREWER, Ebenezer Cobham (1810–97). English writer, author of *A Dictionary of Phrase and Fable.*

BROOME, William (1689–1745), English clergyman, poet and translator.

BROWN, Thomas Edward (1830–97), Manx poet.

BROWNING, Robert (1812–89), English poet.

BURT, Benjamin Hapgood (*b.* 1876), American lyricist and composer.

CAMPBELL, Thomas (1777–1844), Scottish poet.

CARROLL, Lewis (real name Charles Lutwidge Dodgson) (1832–98), English mathematician and writer; author of *Alice in Wonderland* and *Through the Looking-Glass.*

CERVANTES SAAVEDRA, Miguel de (1547–1616), Spanish author of *Don Quixote.*

CHAUCER, Geoffrey (1340?–1400), English author of *The Canterbury Tales.*

CHESTERFIELD, Philip Dormer Stanhope, fourth Earl of (1694–1773), English statesman, famous for his *Letters* to his natural son, Philip Stanhope.

CHESTERTON, Gilbert Keith (1874–1936), English essayist, novelist, poet and critic.

CHURCHILL, Sir Winston Leonard Spencer (1874–1965), English statesman and author.

CICERO, Marcus Tullius (106–43 B.C.), Roman orator.

COBBETT, William (1762–1835), English author and reformer.

COWPER, William (1731–1800), English poet.

CUNNINGHAM, John (1729–73), English poet.

DAVIES, Sir John (1569–1626), English poet.

DRYDEN, John (1631–1700), English poet, dramatist and satirist; Poet Laureate, 1670–89.

DU MAURIER, George (1834–96), British artist and novelist, son of a naturalized Frenchman; author of the novel *Trilby.*

EMERSON, Ralph Waldo (1803–82), American essayist, poet and philosopher.

FITZGERALD, Edward (1809–83), English poet and translator; famous for his translation of *The Rubáiyát of Omar Khayyám*.

FRANKLIN, Benjamin (1706–90), American philosopher and statesman.

FULLER, Thomas (1608–61), English preacher and author.

GAY, John (1685–1732), English poet and dramatist; author of *The Beggar's Opera*.

GIBBON, Edward (1737–94), English historian.

GILBERT, Sir William Schwenck (1836–1911), English dramatist; writer of the librettos of the Gilbert and Sullivan comic operas.

GOLDSMITH, Oliver (1728–74), Irish poet, novelist and dramatist.

GRAY, Thomas (1716–71), English poet.

HERACLITUS (*c.* 540–475 B.C.), Greek philosopher.

HERBERT, George (1593–1633), English poet.

HERRICK, Robert (1591–1674), English poet.

HIPPOCRATES (*c.* 460 B.C.), Greek physician.

HOMER, epic poet of Greece in about the ninth century B.C.

HORACE (Quintus Horatius Flaccus) (65–8 B.C.), Roman poet.

INGALLS, John James (1833–1900), American statesman.

JEFFERSON, Thomas (1743–1826), American statesman.

JEROME, Jerome Klapka (1859–1927), English author.

JOHNSON, Samuel (1709–84), English writer and lexicographer.

KEATS, John (1795–1821), English poet.

KINGSLEY, Charles (1819–75), English cleric, poet and novelist; author of *The Water Babies*.

KIPLING, Rudyard (1865–1936), English writer of verse and fiction.

LEE, Nathaniel (*c.* 1653–92), English dramatist.

LINCOLN, Abraham (1809–65), American statesman.

LONGFELLOW, Henry Wadsworth (1807–82), American poet.

LOUIS XVIII (1755–1824), King of France.

MACKINTOSH, Sir James (1765–1832), Scottish publicist.

MAHOMET (*c.* 570–632), Prophet of Islam.

MASEFIELD, John Edward (1878–1967), English poet, novelist and dramatist; Poet Laureate 1930–67.

MICHELANGELO (1475–1564), Italian artist and sculptor.

MILTON, John (1608–74), English poet and writer.

MOFFATT, James (1870–1944), Scottish divine.

MONTAIGNE, Michel D'Eyquem, Sieur de (1533–92), French essayist.

MORTON, Thomas (1764?–1838), English dramatist.

NAPOLEON BONAPARTE (1769–1821), Emperor of France.

NASHE, Thomas (1567–1601), English writer.

NUGENT, Robert (1702–88), English poet.

OMAR KHAYYÁM (died *c.* 1123), Persian poet. 'Khayyám' means 'tentmaker', i.e. Omar the Tentmaker.

OVID (Publius Ovidus Naso) (43 B.C.–A.D. 17), Roman poet.

OWEN, John (c. 1560–1622), Welsh epigrammatist.

PAYNE, John Howard (1791–1852), American actor and dramatist; author of *Home, Sweet Home.*

PINDAR, Peter (real name John Wolcot) (1738–1819), English satirist.

PLAUTUS, Titus Maccius (c. 251–184 B.C.), Roman dramatist.

PLINY (Gaius Plinius Secundus, known as Pliny the Elder) (c. 23–79), Roman writer.

PLUTARCH (c. 46–120), Greek biographer.

POPE, Alexander (1688–1744), English poet and satirist.

RABELAIS, François (c. 1490–1553/4), French philospher and satirist.

SCOTT, Sir Walter (1771–1832), Scottish novelist and poet.

SENECA, Lucius Annaeus (c. 4 B.C.–A.D. 65), Roman philosopher.

SHAKESPEARE, William (1564–1616), English poet and dramatist.

SIDNEY, Sir Philip (1554–86), English soldier and poet.

SMILES, Samuel (1812–1904), English author.

SMITH, Logan Pearsall (1865–1946), American littérateur living in England.

SMITH, Sydney (1771–1845), English clergyman, author and wit.

SOCRATES (c. 470–399 B.C.), Greek philosopher.

SPURGEON, Charles Haddon (1834–92), English preacher.

STERNE, Laurence (1713–68), English author.

STEVENSON, Robert Louis (1850–94), Scottish author and poet.

SULLIVAN, Sir Arthur Seymour (1842–1900), English composer; composer of the music of the Gilbert and Sullivan comic operas.

SWINBURNE, Algernon Charles (1837–1909), English poet.

TAYLOR, John (1580–1652), English writer.

TENNYSON, Alfred Tennyson, first Baron (1809–92), English poet; Poet Laureate, 1850–92.

THOMPSON, D'Arcy Wentworth (1829–1902), English Greek scholar.

THUCYDIDES (c. 460–c. 400 B.C.), Greek historian.

UNAMUNO, Miguel de (1864–1936), Spanish scholar and man of letters.

VOLTAIRE (real name François Marie Arouet (1694–1778), French philosopher and author.

WALLACE, William Ross (c. 1819–83), American lawyer and writer of verse.

WASHINGTON, George (1732–99), American statesman.

WATTS, Isaac (1674–1748), English hymn writer.

WHITTIER, John Greenleaf (1807–92), American poet.

WILCOX, Ella Wheeler (1855–1919), American poet.

WILSON, John (1627?–96), English playwright.

WITHER, George (1588–1667), English poet.

WORDSWORTH, William (1770–1850), English poet; Poet Laureate, 1843–50.

YOUNG, Edward (1685–1765), English poet.

Index

A

Absence makes the heart grow fonder, 1

Accidents will happen in the best-regulated families, 2

Accuses, accused: He who excuses himself accuses himself, 287; Never ask pardon before you are accused, 484

Aches, aching: Never tell your enemy that your foot aches, 495; The tongue ever turns to the aching tooth, 693

Acorn, acorns: Every oak must be an acorn, 185; Great oaks from little acorns grow, 255

Actions speak louder than words, 3

Adam's ale is the best brew, 4

Adversity: Prosperity makes friends, adversity tries them, 572; Sweet are the uses of adversity, 629

Advice: Advice when most needed is least heeded, 5; Nothing is given so freely as advice, 517

Affairs: There is a tide in the affairs of men . . ., 651

Age: The golden age was never the present age, 244

Agree: Birds in their little nests agree, 53; Two of a trade can never agree, 704

Ale: Adam's ale is the best brew, 4

Alone: He travels the fastest who travels alone, 284; A wise man is never less alone than when he is alone, 766

Angels: Fools rush in where angels fear to tread, 217

Answer: No answer is also an answer, 499; A soft answer turneth away wrath, 605

Appearances; Appearances are deceptive, 19; Never judge by appearances, 487

Apple, apples: The apples on the other side of the wall are the sweetest, 20; The rotten apple injures its neighbours, 590

Art is long, life is short, 21

Ass: Every ass likes to hear himself bray, 170

Astray: Better to ask the way than go astray, 50

B

Baby: Don't empty the baby out with the bath water, 130

Back: Don't make a rod for your own back, 135; The last straw breaks the camel's back, 386; You scratch my back and I'll scratch yours, 797

Bait: The bait hides the hook, 31; The fish will soon be caught that nibbles at every bait, 214

Bargain: Make the best of a bad bargain, 437

Bark, barking: Barking dogs seldom bite, 32; Why keep a dog and bark yourself?, 764

Basket: Don't put all your eggs in one basket, 140

Bath: Don't empty the baby out with the bath water, 130

Battalions: God is always on the side of the big battalions, 240

Battle: The first blow is half the battle, 209

Bear: Catch your bear before you sell its skin, 76

Beauty: Beauty is but skin deep, 35; Beauty is in the eye of the beholder, 36; A thing of beauty is a joy for ever, 675

Bed: As you make your bed, so you must lie in it, 23; Early to bed and early to rise, 157

Beer: Life is not all beer and skittles, 403

Beggar, beggars: Beggars must not be choosers, 37; If wishes were horses, beggars would ride, 330; Set a beggar on horseback and he'll ride to the devil, 597

Begin, begins, beginning, begun: Everything must have a beginning, 190; He who begins many things, finishes but few, 285; He who would climb the ladder must begin at the bottom, 297; Well begun is half done, 723

Believe, believed, believing: A liar is not believed when he tells the truth, 401; Seeing is believing, 594; We soon believe what we desire, 720

Belly: The eye is bigger than the belly, 200; A growing youth has a wolf in his belly, 257

Bend: Better bend than break, 47

Bird, birds: A bird in the hand is worth two in the bush, 52; Birds in their little nests agree, 53; Birds of a feather flock together, 54; The early bird catches the worm, 156; Fine feathers make fine birds, 206; It is a foolish bird that soils its own nest, 347; One beats the bush, and another catches the birds, 527; You cannot catch old birds with chaff, 778

Bite, bites, biter, bitten: Barking dogs seldom bite, 32; The biter is sometimes bit, 55; If you cannot bite never show your teeth, 331; Never make two bites of a cherry, 490; Once bitten, twice shy, 526

Black, blacks: The devil is not so black as he is painted, 112; The pot called the kettle black, 559; There's a black sheep in every flock, 649; Two blacks do not make a white, 700

Blind: If the blind lead the blind, both shall fall into the ditch, 325; In the country of the blind, the one-eyed man is king, 344; Love is blind, 428; Men are blind in their own cause, 454; A nod is as good as a wink to a blind horse, 511; None so blind as those who won't see, 513

Bliss: Where ignorance is bliss, 'tis folly to be wise, 754

Blood: Blood is thicker than water, 57; You cannot get blood out of a stone, 780

Blow: The first blow is half the battle, 209

Bold: Fortune favours the bold, 224

Bone, bones: Sticks and stones may break my bones, but words will never hurt me, 615; Two dogs fight for a bone, and a third runs away with it, 701; What is bred in the bone will never come out of the flesh, 728

Books and friends should be few but good, 58

Borrower: Neither a borrower nor a lender be, 483

Bottles: Do not put new wine into old bottles, 141

Bottom: The best fish swim near the bottom, 38; He who would climb the ladder must begin at the bottom, 297

Bough: Don't cut the bough you are standing on, 129

Boy, boys: All work and no play makes Jack a dull boy, 17; Boys will be boys, 59

Brag: They brag most who can do least, 673

Branch: The highest branch is not the safest roost, 305

Brass: Where there's muck there's brass, 756

Bread: Bread is the staff of life, 60; Don't quarrel with your bread and butter, 143; Half a loaf is better than no bread, 258

Breakfast: If you sing before breakfast, you will cry before night, 334

Brevity is the soul of wit, 61

Bricks: You cannot make bricks without straw, 786

Bridge: Don't cross a bridge till you come to it, 125

Brooms: New brooms sweep clean, 497

Broth: Too many cooks spoil the broth, 695

Build, built: It is easier to pull down than to build, 357: Rome was not built in a day, 588

Bull: The bull must be taken by the horns, 62

Bully: A bully is always a coward, 63

Burn, burns, burnt: Burn not your house to fright the mouse away, 64; A burnt child dreads the fire, 65; Money burns a hole in the pocket, 467; You cannot burn the candle at both ends, 777

Bush: A bird in the hand is worth two in the bush, 52; Good wine needs no bush, 251; One beats the bush, and another catches the birds, 527

Bushel: Hide not your light under a bushel, 304

Busiest men find the most time, 66

Business: Everybody's business is nobody's business, 187

Butter: Don't quarrel with your bread and butter, 143; Fine words butter no parsnips, 207

Butterfly: Take not a musket to kill a butterfly, 633

Buy, buyer: Let the buyer beware, 398; Never buy a pig in a poke, 485

Bygones: Let bygones be bygones, 393

C

Cake: You cannot have your cake and eat it, 782

Calm: After a storm comes a calm, 6

Camel, camels: The last straw breaks the camel's back, 386; Men strain at gnats and swallow camels, 459

Candle: Light not a candle to the sun, 406; You cannot burn the candle at both ends, 777

Canoe: Paddle your own canoe, 551

Cap: If the cap fits, wear it, 326

Care killed a cat, 69

Cart: Don't put the cart before the horse, 142; The worst wheel of the cart creaks most, 775

Cases: Circumstances alter cases, 84

Castle: An Englishman's house is his castle, 166

Cat, cats: All cats are grey in the dark, 8; Care killed a cat, 69; A cat has nine lives, 72; A cat may look at a king, 73; Don't make yourself a mouse, or the cat will eat you, 136; There are more ways of killing a cat than by choking it with cream, 645; When the cat is away the mice will play, 750

Cause: Men are blind in their own cause, 454

Caveat emptor, 77

Certain: Nothing is so certain as the unexpected, 518

Chaff: There is no wheat without chaff, 667; You cannot catch old birds with chaff, 778

Chain: The strength of the chain is in the weakest link, 622

Change: Don't change horses in mid-stream, 123; The leopard cannot change his spots, 392; There is nothing permanent except change, 669; Times change, 689

Charity: Charity begins at home, 78; Charity covers a multitude of sins, 79

Chatters: Who chatters to you will chatter of you, 760

Cheapest: Best is cheapest, 39

Cherchez la femme, 80

Cherry: Never make two bites of a cherry, 490

Chickens: Curses, like chickens, come home to roost, 99; Don't count your chickens before they are hatched, 124

Child, children: A burnt child dreads the fire, 65; The child is father of the man, 81; Children should be seen and not heard, 82; He that hath wife and children hath given hostages to fortune, 277; Spare the rod and spoil the child, 609; When children stand quiet they have done some ill, 743

Christmas comes but once a year, 83

Church: The nearer the church, the farther from God, 479

Circumstances alter cases, 84

City: A great city, a great solitude, 254; If each would sweep before his own door, we should have a clean city, 321

Cleanliness is next to godliness, 85

Clock: One cannot put back the clock, 529

Cloth: Cut your coat according to your cloth, 102

Clothes do not make the man, 86

Cloud, clouds: Every cloud has a silver lining, 171; If there were no clouds, we should not enjoy the sun, 328

Clout: Cast ne'er a clout till May is out, 70

Coat: Cut your coat according to your cloth, 102

Cobbler: Let the cobbler stick to his last, 399

Cock: Every cock crows on his own dunghill, 172; It is a sad house where the hen crows louder than the cock, 351

Command: He that cannot obey cannot command, 271; Through obedience learn to command, 683

Commission: There is a sin of omission as well as of commission, 650

Company: Desert and reward seldom keep company, 107; Good company on the road is the shortest cut, 246; Men are known by the company they keep, 455; Two is company, three is none, 703; Who keeps company with the wolf will learn to howl, 762

Comparisons are odious, 88

Confesses, confessed, confessor, confession: A fault confessed is half redressed, 204; He who denies all confesses all, 286; It is a foolish sheep that makes the wolf his confessor, 348; Open confession is good for the soul, 544

Conscience does make cowards of us all, 89

Consent: Silence gives consent, 601

Constable: Don't outrun the constable, 138

Contempt: Familiarity breeds contempt, 203

Cooks: Too many cooks spoil the broth, 695

Coronets: Kind hearts are more than coronets, 381

Country: God made the country, and man made the town, 241; Happy is the country that has no history, ?62; In the country of the blind, the one-eyed man is king, 344; The prophet is not without honour, save in his own country, and in his own house, 571; So many countries, so many customs, 604

Courage: Many would be cowards if they had courage enough, 449

Course: The course of true love never did run smooth, 93; Safety lies in the middle course, 591

Courtesy: Courtesy costs nothing, 94; Full of courtesy, full of craft, 228

Coverlet: Stretch your legs according to your coverlet, 623

Cow: You cannot sell the cow and drink the milk, 789

Coward, cowards: A bully is always a coward, 63; Conscience does make cowards of us all, 89; Cowards die many times before their deaths, 95; Many would be cowards if they had courage enough, 449

Cowl: The cowl does not make the monk, 96

Crab: You cannot make a crab walk straight, 783

Cradle: The hand that rocks the cradle rules the world, 260

Craft: Full of courtesy, full of craft, 228

Cream: There are more ways of killing a cat than by choking it with cream, 645

Credit: Give credit where credit is due, 234

Cross: No cross, no crown, 500

Crown: No cross, no crown, 500

Crutches: One foot is better than two crutches, 530

Cup: The last drop makes the cup run over, 385; There's many a slip 'twixt the cup and the lip, 655

Cupboard: Every family has a skeleton in the cupboard, 174

Cure, cured: Prevention is better than cure, 566; What can't be cured must be endured, 725

Curiosity: Too much curiosity lost Paradise, 696

Curses: Curses, like chickens, come home to roost, 99; Water is a boon in the desert, but the drowning man curses it, 717

Custom, customs: Custom makes all things easy, 100; Custom reconciles us to everything, 101; So many countries, so many customs, 604

D

Danger, dangerous: A little learning is a dangerous thing, 417; Out of debt, out of danger, 549; The thin end of the wedge is dangerous, 674

Dark, darkest: All cats are grey in the dark, 8; The darkest hour is that before the dawn, 103

Daughter: He that would the daughter win, must with the mother first begin, 283

Dawn: The darkest hour is that before the dawn, 103

Day, days: Every dog has his day, 173; He that fights and runs away may live to fight another day, 273; Keep something for a rainy day, 379; The longest day must have an end, 424; One of these days is none of these days, 538; Rome was not built in a day, 588; Sufficient unto the day is the evil thereof, 627; Tomorrow is another day, 691; A wonder lasts but nine days, 769

Dead: Call no man happy till he is dead, 68; Dead men tell no tales, 104; It is ill waiting for dead men's shoes, 363; It is useless to flog a dead horse, 370; Queen Anne is dead, 577; Speak well of the dead, 612

Deaf: None so deaf as those who won't hear, 514

Death, deaths: Cowards die many times before their deaths, 95; Death is the great leveller, 105

Debt: Out of debt, out of danger, 549

Deceives: If a man deceives me once, shame on him; if he deceives me twice, shame on me, 318

Deceptive: Appearances are deceptive, 19

Deed, deeds: Deeds, not words, 106; A man of words and not of deeds is like a garden full of weeds, 442; Take the will for the deed, 636

Deep: Still waters run deep, 617

Defects: Every man has the defects of his own virtues, 182

Delays: Desires are nourished by delays, 108

Denies: He who denies all confesses all, 286

Desert (wilderness): Water is a boon in the desert, but the drowning man curses it, 717; (worthiness): Desert and reward seldom keep company, 107

Desire, desires: Desires are nourished by delays, 108; We soon believe what we desire, 720

Devil: Better the devil you know than the devil you don't know, 49; The devil can cite Scripture for his purpose, 110; The devil finds work for idle hands to do, 111; The devil is not so black as he is painted, 112; The devil was sick . . ., 114; Every man for himself, and the devil take the hindmost, 180; Give the devil his due, 236; He should have a long spoon that sups with the devil, 270; Needs must when the devil drives, 482; Set a beggar on horseback and he'll ride to the devil, 597; Speak the truth and shame the devil, 611; Talk of the devil and he is sure to appear, 641

Diamond cut diamond, 115

Die, dying: Dying is as natural as living, 155; A man can only die once, 440; Never say die, 492; Those whom the gods love die young, 681

Difficult: All things are difficult before they are easy, 16

Dirt, dirty: Fling dirt enough and some will stick, 215; Don't wash your dirty linen in public, 149

Discontent is the first step in progress, 116

Discretion: Discretion is the better part of valour, 117; An ounce of discretion is worth a pound of wit, 548

Disease, diseases: Desperate diseases must have desperate remedies, 109; The purse of the patient protracts the disease, 575; The remedy may be worse than the disease, 582

Distance: Distance lends enchantment to the view, 118; Respect is greater from a distance, 583

Ditch: If one sheep leaps over the ditch, all the rest will follow, 324; If the blind lead the blind, both shall fall into the ditch, 325

Divided: A house divided against itself cannot stand, 314; United we stand, divided we fall, 707

Dog, dogs: All are not thieves that dogs bark at, 7; Barking dogs seldom bite, 32; Better be the head of a dog than the tail of a lion, 46; Dog does not eat dog, 151; Every dog has his day, 173; Give a dog a bad name and hang him, 230; Help a lame dog over a stile, 302; Let sleeping dogs lie, 397; Love me, love my dog, 431; Two dogs fight for a bone, and a third runs away with it, 701; Why keep a dog and bark yourself?, 764; You cannot teach an old dog new tricks, 791

Dogged: It's dogged that does it, 356

Door: A door must be either shut or open, 152; A golden key opens every door, 245; If each would sweep before his own door, we should have a clean city, 321; When one door shuts another opens, 749; When the wolf comes in at the door, love creeps out of the window, 751

Doubt: When in doubt do nowt, 746; When in doubt leave out, 747

Drink: You cannot sell the cow and drink the milk, 789; You may lead a horse to the water, but you cannot make him drink, 793

Drop: The last drop makes the cup run over, 385

Drunkenness: What soberness conceals, drunkenness reveals, 738

Due: Give credit where credit is due, 234; Give the devil his due, 236

Dunghill: Every cock crows on his own dunghill, 172; The sun is never the worse for shining on a dunghill, 628

Dwarf: A dwarf on a giant's shoulders sees the farther of the two, 154

E

Ear, ears: Little pitchers have long ears, 418; Walls have ears, 713; You cannot make a silk purse out of a sow's ear, 784

Early: The early bird catches the worm, 156; Early to bed and early to rise, 157

East or west, home is best, 159

Easy, easier: All things are difficult before they are easy, 16; Custom makes all things easy, 100; Easier said than done, 158; Easy come, easy go, 160; It is easier to pull down than to build, 357; It is easy to be wise after the event, 358; It is easy to bear the misfortunes of others, 359

Eavesdroppers never hear any good of themselves, 161

Ebb: Every flow must have its ebb, 175

Egg, eggs: Better an egg today than a hen tomorrow, 42; Don't put all your eggs in one basket, 140; Don't teach your grandmother to suck eggs, 147; He that would have eggs must endure the cackling of hens, 282; Kill not the goose that lays the golden eggs, 380; You cannot make an omelet without breaking eggs, 785

Eleven: Rain before seven, fine before eleven, 578

Enchantment: Distance lends enchantment to the view, 118

End, ends: All good things come to an end, 9; All's well that ends well, 12; The end justifies the means, 164; The end makes all equal, 165; The longest day must have an end, 424; The thin end of the wedge is dangerous, 674; You cannot burn the candle at both ends, 777

Endured: What can't be cured must be endured, 725

Enemy, enemies: The best is often the enemy of the good, 40; Every man is his own worst enemy, 183; May God defend me from my friends; I can defend myself from my enemies, 453; Never tell your enemy that your foot aches, 495

Englishman: An Englishman's house is his castle, 166

Err: To err is human, 690

Event, events: Coming events cast their shadows before, 87; It is easy to be wise after the event, 358

Everything: Everything comes to him who waits, 189; Everything must have a beginning, 190; A place for everything, and everything in its place, 556

Evil, evils: Evil be to him who evil thinks, 191; The love of money is the root of all evil, 432; Of two evils choose the lesser, 524; Sufficient unto the day is the evil thereof, 627

Example is better than precept, 192

Exception: The exception proves the rule, 193

Exchange is no robbery, 194

Excuse, excuses: He who excuses himself accuses himself, 287; An ill payer never wants an excuse, 338

Expect, expects, expectation: Blessed is he who expects nothing, for he shall never be disappointed, 56; Expectation is better than realization, 195; What can you expect from a hog but a grunt?, 724

Experience: Experience is the mother of wisdom, 196; Experience is the teacher of fools, 197

Extremes meet, 198

Eye, eyed: Beauty is in the eye of the beholder, 36; An eye for an eye, and a tooth for a tooth, 199; The eye is bigger than the belly, 200; Hew not too high lest the chips fall in thine eye, 303; In the country of the blind, the one-eyed man is king, 344; What the eye doesn't see the heart doesn't grieve over, 739

F

Face: Don't cut off your nose to spite your face, 128; A man without a smiling face must not open a shop, 444

Faint heart ne'er won fair lady, 201

Familiarity breeds contempt, 203

Family, families: Accidents will happen in the best-regulated families, 2; Every family has a skeleton in the cupboard, 174

Fashion: He who goes against the fashion is himself its slave, 289

Fat: Laugh and grow fat, 387

Father: The child is father of the man, 81; Like father, like son, 409; The wish is father to the thought, 768

Fault, faults: A fault confessed is half redressed, 204; He that commits a fault thinks everyone speaks of it, 272; Know your own faults before blaming others for theirs, 382

Feast: A contented mind is a perpetual feast, 92; Enough is as good as a feast, 167

Feather, feathers: Birds of a feather flock together, 54; Fine feathers make fine birds, 206

Fence, fences: Good fences make good neighbours, 247; Love your neighbour, yet pull not down your fence, 434

Fiction: Truth is stranger than fiction, 698

Fiddle: It needs more skill than I can tell to play the second fiddle well, 371; There's many a good tune played on an old fiddle, 654

Fight, fights: He that fights and runs away may live to fight another day, 273; Two dogs fight for a bone, and a third runs away with it, 701

Find, finding: Finding's keeping, 205; Nothing seek, nothing find, 519; Take things as you find them, 638

Fingers were made before forks, 208

Fire: A burnt child dreads the fire, 65; Do not have too many irons in the fire, 132; Pouring oil on the fire is not the way to quench it, 560; There is no smoke without fire, 665

Fish, fishing: All's fish that comes to the net, 11; The best fish swim near the bottom, 38; Don't cry stinking fish, 127; The fish will soon be caught that nibbles at every bait, 214; It is good fishing in troubled waters, 360; There are as good fish in the sea as ever came out of it, 644

Flattery: Imitation is the sincerest form of flattery, 340

Flesh: The spirit is willing, but the flesh is weak, 614; What is bred in the bone will never come out of the flesh, 728

Flock: Birds of a feather flock together, 54; There's a black sheep in every flock, 649

Flow: Every flow must have its ebb, 175

Fly, flies: Make yourself all honey and the flies will devour you, 439; You must lose a fly to catch a trout, 795

Folly: Where ignorance is bliss, 'tis folly to be wise, 754

Fool, fools, foolish: Better be a fool than a knave, 43; Experience is the teacher of fools, 197; A fool and his money are soon parted, 216; Fools rush in where angels fear to tread, 217; It is a foolish sheep that makes the wolf his confessor, 348; More know Tom Fool than Tom Fool knows, 471; There's no fool like an old fool, 658; Wise men learn by other men's mistakes; fools by their own, 767

Foot: Never tell your enemy that your foot aches, 495; One foot is better than two crutches, 530

Footprints on the sands of time are not made by sitting down, 218

Forbidden fruit is sweetest, 220
Forearmed: Forewarned is forearmed, 222
Forelock: Ţake time by the forelock, 639
Forewarned is forearmed, 222
Forgive and forget, 223
Forks: Fingers were made before forks, 208
Fortune: Fortune favours the bold, 224; Fortune knocks at least once at
   every man's gate, 225; He that hath wife and children hath given hostages to fortune, 277
Friend, friends: The best of friends must part, 41; Books and friends
   should be few but good, 58; A friend in need is a friend indeed, 226; He
   that hath a full purse never wanted a friend, 275; Lend your money and
   lose your friend, 391; May God defend me from my friends; I can defend
   myself from my enemies, 453; Prosperity makes friends, adversity tries
   them, 572; Success has many friends, 626; When I lent I had a friend;
   when I asked he was unkind, 745
Friendship: A hedge between keeps friendship green, 301
Fruit: Forbidden fruit is sweetest, 220; A tree is known by its fruit, 697
Funny: A rich man's joke is always funny, 585

G

Gain: No gain without pain, 501
Game: Lookers-on see most of the game, 427
Gander: What is sauce for the goose is sauce for the gander, 730
Garden: A man of words and not of deeds is like a garden full of weeds,
   442; There is no garden without its weeds, 659
Gate: A creaking gate hangs long, 97; Fortune knocks at least once at
   every man's gate, 225
Gath: Tell it not in Gath . . ., 643
Generous: Be just before you are generous, 33
Giant: A dwarf on a giant's shoulders sees the farther of the two, 154
Gift: Never look a gift horse in the mouth, 488
Glass: Those who live in glass houses should not throw stones, 680
Gluttony kills more than the sword, 238
Gnats: Men strain at gnats and swallow camels, 459
God: God helps those who help themselves, 239; God is always on the
   side of the big battalions, 240; God made the country, and man made
   the town, 241; God tempers the wind to the shorn lamb, 242; Man
   proposes, God disposes, 443; May God defend me from my friends; I
   can defend myself from my enemies, 453; The mills of God grind slowly,
   462; The nearer the church, the farther from God, 479; The voice of the
   people is the voice of God, 711; You cannot serve God and mammon, 790

Godliness: Cleanliness is next to godliness, 85

Gods: The gods send nuts to those who have no teeth, 243; Those whom the gods love die young, 681

Gold: All that glitters is not gold, 15

Golden: The golden age was never the present age, 244; A golden key opens every door, 245; Kill not the goose that lays the golden eggs, 380; Speech is silver, silence is golden, 613

Goose: Kill not the goose that lays the golden eggs, 380; What is sauce for the goose is sauce for the gander, 730

Grandmother: Don't teach your grandmother to suck eggs, 147

Grapes: The grapes are sour, 252

Grasp all, lose all, 253

Grass: Take heed of the snake in the grass, 632

Greek: When Greek meets Greek, then comes the tug of war, 744

Grin: You must grin and bear it, 794

Grist: All's grist that comes to the mill, 11

Grundy: What will Mrs Grundy say?, 740

Grunt: What can you expect from a hog but a grunt?, 724

Guest: A constant guest is never welcome, 91

Gutters: Who repairs not his gutters repairs his whole house, 763

H

Handsome is as handsome does, 261

Happy: Call no man happy till he is dead, 68; Happy is the country that has no history, 262

Hardship: Through hardship to the stars, 682

Hare, hares: First catch your hare, 210; If you run after two hares you will catch neither, 333; You cannot run with the hare and hunt with the hounds, 788

Harp: Don't take your harp to the party, 146; Harp not for ever on the same string, 263; Not good is it to harp on the frayed string, 515

Haste: Haste makes waste, 264; Haste trips over its own heels, 265; Make haste slowly, 435; Marry in haste, and repent at leisure, 452; More haste, less speed, 470

Hay: Make hay while the sun shines, 436

Head, heads: Better be the head of a dog than the tail of a lion, 46; A still tongue makes a wise head, 616; Two heads are better than one, 702; Uneasy lies the head that wears a crown, 706; You cannot put old heads on young shoulders, 787

Healer: Time is the great healer, 688

Health is better than wealth, 298

Heart, hearts: Absence makes the heart grow fonder, 1; Faint heart ne'er won fair lady, 201; A heavy purse makes a light heart, 300; Hope deferred maketh the heart sick, 311; If it were not for hope, the heart would break, 323; It is a sad heart that never rejoices, 350; Kind hearts are more than coronets, 381; A light purse makes a heavy heart, 407; The way to a man's heart is through his stomach, 718; What the eye doesn't see the heart doesn't grieve over, 739

Heaven: Heaven helps those who help themselves, 299; Marriages are made in heaven, 451

Hedge: A hedge between keeps friendship green, 301; Men leap over where the hedge is lowest, 457

Heels: Haste trips over its own heels, 265; One pair of heels is often worth two pairs of hands, 539

Hell: The road to hell is paved with good intentions, 586

Help, helps: Every little helps, 179; God helps those who help themselves, 239; Help a lame dog over a stile, 302; A little help is worth a deal of pity, 416

Hen, hens: Better an egg today than a hen tomorrow, 42; He that would have eggs must endure the cackling of hens, 282; It is a sad house where the hen crows louder than the cock, 351

Hero: No man is a hero to his valet, 503

Hesitates: He who hesitates is lost, 291

Hire: The labourer is worthy of his hire, 384

History: Happy is the country that has no history, 262; History repeats itself, 306

Hog: What can you expect from a hog but a grunt?, 724

Home, homes: Charity begins at home, 78; Curses, like chickens, come home to roost, 99; East or west, home is best, 159; The longest way round is the nearest way home, 425; Men make houses, women make homes, 458; The shortest way round is the longest way home, 600; There's no place like home, 661

Homer: Even Homer sometimes nods, 169

Honest, honesty: Honesty is the best policy, 309; When thieves fall out, honest men come by their own, 753

Honey: Make yourself all honey and the flies will devour you, 439

Honour: A prophet is not without honour, save in his own country, and in his own house, 571; There is honour among thieves, 653

Hook: The bait hides the hook, 31

Hope: Hope deferred maketh the heart sick, 311; Hope for the best and prepare for the worst, 312; Hope springs eternal in the human breast, 313; If it were not for hope, the heart would break, 323; While there is life there is hope, 759

Horse, horses: All lay loads on a willing horse, 13; Don't change horses in mid-stream, 123; Don't put the cart before the horse, 142; Don't ride the high horse, 144; Every horse thinks its own pack heaviest, 176; If two men ride on a horse, one must ride behind, 329; If wishes were horses, beggars would ride, 330; It is too late to lock the stable when the horse has been stolen, 369; It is useless to flog a dead horse, 370; Never look a gift horse in the mouth, 488; Never spur a willing horse, 494; A nod is as good as a wink to a blind horse, 511; Put the saddle on the right horse, 576; You may lead a horse to the water, but you cannot make him drink, 793; Zeal without knowledge is a runaway horse, 800

Horseback: Set a beggar on horseback and he'll ride to the devil, 597

Hounds: You cannot run with the hare and hunt with the hounds, 788

Hour, hours: The darkest hour is that before the dawn, 103; Pleasant hours fly fast, 557

House, houses: Burn not your house to fright the mouse away, 64; An Englishman's house is his castle, 166; A house divided against itself cannot stand, 314; It is a sad house where the hen crows louder than the cock, 351; Men make houses, women make homes, 458; A prophet is not without honour, save in his own country, and in his own house, 571; Those who live in glass houses should not throw stones, 680; Who repairs not his gutters repairs his whole house, 763

Hunger is the best sauce, 315

Husband: A good husband makes a good wife, 248

Hypocrisy is a homage that vice pays to virtue, 316

I

Ignorance: Where ignorance is bliss, 'tis folly to be wise, 754

Imitation is the sincerest form of flattery, 340

Impressions: First impressions are most lasting, 212

Inch, inches: Give knaves an inch and they will take a yard, 235; Men are not to be measured in inches, 456

Indispensable: No man is indispensable, 505

Industry: Want is the mother of industry, 714

Infallible: No man is infallible, 506

Inspiration: Ninety per cent of inspiration is perspiration, 498

Intentions: The road to hell is paved with good intentions, 586

Invention: Necessity is the mother of invention, 480

Iron, irons: Don't have too many irons in the fire, 132; Strike while the iron is hot, 624

J

Jack: All work and no play makes Jack a dull boy, 17; A Jack of all trades is master of none, 376; Every Jack must have his Jill, 177

Jam tomorrow and jam yesterday – but never jam today, 377

Jest, jesting: It is ill jesting with edged tools, 361; There's many a true word spoken in jest, 656

Job: Give us the tools, and we will finish the job, 237; Make the best of a bad job, 438

Joke: A rich man's joke is always funny, 585

Joy: A thing of beauty is a joy for ever, 675

Judge: Judge not, that ye be not judged, 378; Never judge by appearances, 487

Just: Be just before you are generous, 33

K

Kernel: He that would eat the kernel must crack the nut, 281

Kettle: The pot called the kettle black, 559

Key: A golden key opens every door, 245

Kin: One touch of nature makes the whole world kin, 541

Kind, kindness: A forced kindness deserves no thanks, 221; Kind hearts are more than coronets, 381

King, kings: A cat may look at a king, 73; In the country of the blind, the one-eyed man is king, 344; Punctuality is the politeness of kings, 574

Kiss: Many kiss the hand they wish to cut off, 448

Knave, knaves: Better be a fool than a knave, 43; Give knaves an inch and they will take a yard, 235

Knowledge: Knowledge is power, 383; Zeal without knowledge is a runaway horse, 800

L

Labourer: The labourer is worthy of his hire, 384

Ladder: He who would climb the ladder must begin at the bottom, 297

Lady: Faint heart ne'er won fair lady, 201

Lamb: As well be hanged for a sheep as a lamb, 22; God tempers the wind to the shorn lamb, 242

Lane: It is a long lane that has no turning, 349

Last: Let the cobbler stick to his last, 399

Late: Better late than never, 48; It is never too late to mend, 365; It is too late to lock the stable when the horse has been stolen, 369

Laugh, laughs: He laughs best who laughs last, 269; Laugh and grow fat, 387; Laugh and the world laughs with you, weep and you weep alone, 388; Love laughs at locksmiths, 429

Law: Every law has a loophole, 178; Necessity knows no law, 481; Possession is nine points of the law, 558; Self-preservation is the first law of nature, 596

Learn, learning: Learn to walk before you run, 389; A little learning is a dangerous thing, 417; Live and learn, 421; One is never too old to learn, 532; There is no royal road to learning, 664; Through obedience learn to command, 683; Who keeps company with the wolf will learn to howl, 762

Legs: Stretch your legs according to your coverlet, 623

Leisure: Idle folk have the least leisure, 317; Marry in haste, and repent at leisure, 452

Lend, lent, lender: Lend your money and lose your friend, 391; Neither a borrower nor a lender be, 483; When I lent I had a friend; when I asked he was unkind, 745

Leopard: The leopard cannot change his spots, 392

Lie, lies, liar, liars: Ask no questions and be told no lies, 25; Give a lie twenty-four hours' start and you can never overtake it, 231; A liar is not believed when he tells the truth, 401; Liars should have good memories, 402; One lie makes many, 533

Life, lives: Art is long, life is short, 21; Bread is the staff of life, 60; A cat has nine lives, 72; Life is not all beer and skittles, 403; Life is short and time is swift, 404; Life is sweet, 405; Variety is the spice of life, 708; While there is life there is hope, 759

Light: Hide not your light under a bushel, 304

Line: One must draw the line somewhere, 537

Linen: Don't wash your dirty linen in public, 149

Lining: Every cloud has a silver lining, 171

Lion: Better be the head of a dog than the tail of a lion, 46; A lion may come to be beholden to a mouse, 412; Wake not a sleeping lion, 712

Lip: There's many a slip 'twixt the cup and the lip, 655

Live, lives, living: Dying is as natural as living, 155; Half the world knows not how the other half lives, 259; Live and learn, 421; Live and let live, 422; Live not to eat, but eat to live, 423; Those who live in glass houses should not throw stones, 680

Loaf: Half a loaf is better than no bread, 258

Locksmiths: Love laughs at locksmiths, 429

Loophole: Every law has a loophole, 178

Lot: No man is content with his lot, 504

Lottery: Marriage is a lottery, 450

Love: All's fair in love and war, 10; The course of true love never did run smooth, 93; It is love that makes the world go round, 364; Love is blind, 428; Love laughs at locksmiths, 429; Love me little, love me long, 430; Love me, love my dog, 431; The love of money is the root of all evil, 432; Love will find a way, 433; Love your neighbour, yet pull not down your

fence, 434; Those whom the gods love die young, 681; When the wolf comes in at the door, love creeps out of the window, 751
Luck: The worse luck now, the better another time, 773
Lump: If you don't like it you may lump it, 332

M

Mackerel: Throw out a sprat to catch a mackerel, 684
Mahomet: If the mountain will not come to Mahomet, Mahomet must go to the mountain, 327
Mammon: You cannot serve God and mammon, 790
Manners: Manners maketh man, 445; Other times, other manners, 547
Marriage, marriages, marry: Marriage is a lottery, 450; Marriages are made in heaven, 451; Marry in haste, and repent at leisure, 452
Master, masters: A Jack of all trades is master of none, 376; Like master, like man, 410; No man can serve two masters, 502
May: Cast ne'er a clout till May is out, 70
Means: The end justifies the means, 164
Meat: One man's meat is another man's poison, 535
Medal: Every medal has two sides, 184
Might, mightier: Might is right, 460; The pen is mightier than the sword, 553
Mile: A miss is as good as a mile, 464
Milk: It is no use crying over spilt milk, 366; You cannot sell the cow and drink the milk, 789
Mill: All's grist that comes to the mill, 11; A mill cannot grind with the water that is past, 461; The mills of God grind slowly, 462
Mind, minds: A contented mind is a perpetual feast, 92; Little things please little minds, 420; Out of sight, out of mind, 550
Misfortunes: It is easy to bear the misfortunes of others, 359; Misfortunes never come singly, 463
Mistakes: He who makes no mistakes makes nothing, 292; Wise men learn by other men's mistakes; fools by their own, 767
Moderation in all things, 465
Molehill: Don't make a mountain out of a molehill, 134
Money: A fool and his money are soon parted, 216; Lend your money and lose your friend, 391; The love of money is the root of all evil, 432; Money begets money, 466; Money burns a hole in the pocket, 467; Money talks, 469; Muck and money go together, 476; Never spend your money before you have it, 493; Time is money, 687
Monk: The cowl does not make the monk, 96
Moss: A rolling stone gathers no moss, 587

Mother: Experience is the mother of wisdom, 196; He that would the daughter win, must with the mother first begin, 283; Necessity is the mother of invention, 480; Want is the mother of industry, 714

Mountain: Don't make a mountain out of a molehill, 134; If the mountain will not come to Mahomet, Mahomet must go to the mountain, 327

Mouse, mice: Burn not your house to fright the mouse away, 64; Don't make yourself a mouse, or the cat will eat you, 136; A lion may come to be beholden to a mouse, 412; The mouse that has but one hole is quickly taken, 474; When the cat is away the mice will play, 750

Muck: Muck and money go together, 476; Where there's muck there's brass, 756

Murder will out, 477

Musket: Take not a musket to kill a butterfly, 633

N

Nail: For want of a nail . . ., 219

Name, names: Give a dog a bad name and hang him, 230; A good name is sooner lost than won, 249; No names, no pack drill, 507; A rose by any other name would smell as sweet. 589

Nature: Nature abhors a vacuum, 478; One touch of nature makes the whole world kin, 541; Self-preservation is the first law of nature, 596

Necessity: Necessity is the mother of invention, 480; Necessity knows no law, 481

Need, needs: A friend in need is a friend indeed, 226; Needs must when the devil drives, 482

Neighbour, neighbours: Good fences make good neighbours, 247; Love your neighbour, yet pull not down your fence, 434; The rotten apple injures its neighbours, 590

Nest, nests: Birds in their little nests agree, 53; It is a foolish bird that fouls its own nest, 347

Net: All's fish that comes to the net, 11

Nettle: He who handles a nettle tenderly is soonest stung, 290

News: Bad news travels fast, 27; Ill news comes apace, 337; No news is good news, 508

Night: If you sing before breakfast, you will cry before night, 334; Red sky at night . . ., 581

Noblesse oblige, 509

Nod, nods: Even Homer sometimes nods, 169; A nod is as good as a wink, 510; A nod is as good as a wink to a blind horse, 511

Nose: Don't cut off your nose to spite your face, 128; He that has a great nose thinks everybody is speaking of it, 274

Numbers: There is safety in numbers, 671

Nut, nuts: The gods send nuts to those who have no teeth, 243; He that would eat the kernel must crack the nut, 281

O

Oak, oaks: Every oak must be an acorn, 185; Great oaks from little acorns grow, 255; Little strokes fell great oaks, 419

Oats: The young will sow their wild oats, 798

Obey, obedience: He that cannot obey cannot command, 271; Through obedience learn to command, 683

Oil: Pouring oil on the fire is not the way to quench it, 560

Omelet: You cannot make an omelet without breaking eggs, 785

Omission: There is a sin of omission as well as of commission, 650

Opinion: We are all slaves of opinion, 719

Opportunity: Opportunity makes the thief, 545; Opportunity seldom knocks twice, 546

P

Pack: Every horse thinks its own pack heaviest, 176; No names, no pack drill, 507

Paddle your own canoe, 551

Padlock: Wedlock is a padlock, 722

Pain: No gain without pain, 501; There is no pleasure without pain, 662

Paradise: Too much curiosity lost Paradise, 696

Pardon: Never ask pardon before you are accused, 484

Parsnips: Fine words butter no parsnips, 207

Party: Don't take your harp to the party, 146

Patience, patient: Patience is a virtue, 552; The purse of the patient protracts the disease, 575

Peace: If you want peace, prepare for war, 336; There is no peace for the wicked, 660

Pearls: Do not cast your pearls before swine, 122

Pen: The pen is mightier than the sword, 553

Penny, pence: A bad penny always comes back, 28; In for a penny, in for a pound, 342; Take care of the pence and the pounds will take care of themselves, 631

People: The voice of the people is the voice of God, 711

Per ardua ad astra, 554

Permanent: There is nothing permanent except change, 669

Perspiration: Ninety per cent of inspiration is perspiration, 498

Pie-crust: Promises are like pie-crust, made to be broken, 568

Pig: Never buy a pig in a poke, 485
Pilot: In a calm sea every man is a pilot, 341
Pint: You cannot get a quart into a pint pot, 779
Piper: He who pays the piper calls the tune, 293
Pitch: He that toucheth pitch shall be defiled, 279
Pitcher, pitchers: Little pitchers have long ears, 418; The pitcher goes so often to the well that it is broken at last, 555; Whether the pitcher strikes the stone, or the stone the pitcher, it is bad for the pitcher, 758
Pity: A little help is worth a deal of pity, 416
Place, places: One cannot be in two places at once, 528; A place for everything, and everything in its place, 556; There's no place like home, 661
Pleasure, pleasures: Stolen pleasures are sweetest, 620; There is no pleasure without pain, 662
Poacher: An old poacher makes the best keeper, 525
Pocket: Money burns a hole in the pocket, 467
Poison: One man's meat is another man's poison, 535
Policy: Honesty is the best policy, 309
Politeness: Punctuality is the politeness of kings, 574
Port: Any port in a storm, 18
Possession is nine points of the law, 558
Pot, pots: If 'ifs' and 'ans' were pots and pans . . ., 322; The pot called the kettle black, 559; Praise without profit puts little in the pot, 565; A watched pot never boils, 716; You cannot get a quart into a pint pot, 779
Pound, pounds: In for a penny, in for a pound, 342; An ounce of discretion is worth a pound of wit, 548; Take care of the pence and the pounds will take care of themselves, 631
Poverty is no sin, 561
Power: Knowledge is power, 383
Practice makes perfect, 562
Practise what you preach, 563
Praise: Praise makes good men better and bad men worse, 564; Praise without profit puts little in the pot, 565; Self-praise is no recommendation, 595
Preach: Practise what you preach, 563
Precept: Example is better than precept, 192
Present: The golden age was never the present age, 244; There is no time like the present, 666
Prevention is better than cure, 566
Price: Every man has his price, 181; A thing you don't want is dear at any price, 676
Pricks: Do not kick against the pricks, 133
Procrastination is the thief of time, 567
Profit: Praise without profit puts little in the pot, 565
Progress: Discontent is the first step in progress, 116

Promises are like pie-crust, made to be broken, 568

Proof, proves: The proof of the pudding is in the eating, 569; The exception proves the rule, 193

Prophet: A prophet is not without honour, save in his own country, and in his own house, 571

Prosperity makes friends, adversity tries them, 572

Providence is always on the side of the big battalions, 573

Public: Don't wash your dirty linen in public, 149

Pudding: The proof of the pudding is in the eating, 569

Punctuality is the politeness of kings, 574

Purse: He that hath a full purse never wanted a friend, 275; He that hath not silver in his purse should have silk in his tongue, 276; A heavy purse makes a light heart, 300; A light purse makes a heavy heart, 407; Little and often fills the purse, 414; The purse of the patient protracts the disease, 575; You cannot make a silk purse out of a sow's ear, 784

Q

Quarrel: Don't quarrel with your bread and butter, 143; It takes two to make a quarrel, 374

Quart: You cannot get a quart into a pint pot, 779

Queen Anne is dead, 577

Question, questions, questioner: Ask no questions and be told no lies, 25; Avoid a questioner, for he is also a tattler, 26; There are two sides to every question, 647

R

Race: Slow but sure wins the race, 603

Rain, rains, rainy: It never rains but it pours, 372; Keep something for a rainy day, 379; Rain before seven, fine before eleven, 578

Rats desert a sinking ship, 579

Realization: Expectation is better than realization, 195

Reap, reaps: As you sow, so shall you reap, 24; One man sows and another reaps, 534; Sow the wind and reap the whirlwind, 608

Recommendation: Self-praise is no recommendation, 595

Receiver: The receiver is as bad as the thief, 580

Red sky at night . . ., 581

Remedy, remedies: Desperate diseases must have desperate remedies, 109; The remedy may be worse than the disease, 582

Repent: Marry in haste, and repent at leisure, 452

Reproach: The sting of a reproach is the truth of it, 618

Respect is greater from a distance, 583

Revenge is sweet, 584

Reward: Desert and reward seldom keep company, 107; Virtue is its own reward, 710

Rich: He is rich that has few wants, 268; A rich man's joke is always funny, 585

Ridiculous: From the sublime to the ridiculous is but a step, 227

Right: Might is right, 460; Two wrongs do not make a right, 705

Road, roads: All roads lead to Rome, 14; The beaten road is the safest, 34; Good company on the road is the shortest cut, 246; The road to hell is paved with good intentions, 586; There is no royal road to learning, 664

Robbery: Exchange is no robbery, 194

Rod: Don't make a rod for your own back, 135; Spare the rod and spoil the child, 609

Rome: All roads lead to Rome, 14; Rome was not built in a day, 588; When in Rome do as the Romans do, 748

Roost: Curses, like chickens, come home to roost, 99; The highest branch is not the safest roost, 305

Rope: Give a thief enough rope and he'll hang himself, 232

Rose: The fairest rose is at last withered, 202; A rose by any other name would smell as sweet, 589; There is no rose without a thorn, 663

Rosebuds: Gather ye rosebuds while ye may, 229

Rough: Take the rough with the smooth, 635

Roundabouts: What one loses on the swings one makes up on the roundabouts, 737

Royal: There is no royal road to learning, 664

Rule: The exception proves the rule, 193

Rust: It is better to wear out than to rust out, 355

S

Sack: An empty sack cannot stand upright, 162; You may know by a handful the whole sack, 792

Saddle: Put the saddle on the right horse, 576

Safety: Safety lies in the middle course, 591; There is safety in numbers, 671

Sauce: Hunger is the best sauce, 315; What is sauce for the goose is sauce for the gander, 730

School: Don't tell tales out of school, 148

Scratch: You scratch my back and I'll scratch yours, 797

Scripture: The devil can cite Scripture for his purpose, 110

Sea: In a calm sea every man a is pilot, 341; There are as good fish in the sea as ever came out of it, 644; Worse things happen at sea, 774

Seek: Nothing seek, nothing find, 519

Self-praise is no recommendation, 595

Self-preservation is the first law of nature, 596

Seven: Rain before seven, fine before eleven, 578

Shadow, shadows: Catch not at the shadow and lose the substance, 75; Coming events cast their shadows before, 87

Shame: If a man deceives me once, shame on him; if he deceives me twice, shame on me, 318; Speak the truth and shame the devil, 611

Share and share alike, 599

Shearer: A bad shearer never had a good sickle, 29

Sheep: As well be hanged for a sheep as a lamb, 22; If one sheep leaps over the ditch, all the rest will follow, 324; It is a foolish sheep that makes the wolf his confessor, 348; There's a black sheep in every flock, 649

Ship: It is no use spoiling the ship for a ha'p'orth of tar, 367; Rats desert a sinking ship, 579

Shoe, shoes: It is ill waiting for dead men's shoes, 363; Only the wearer knows where the shoe pinches, 543

Shoemaker: Who is worse shod than the shoemaker's wife?, 761

Shop: A man without a smiling face must not open a shop, 444

Shoulders: A dwarf on a giant's shoulders sees the farther of the two, 154; You cannot put old heads on young shoulders, 787

Sickle: A bad shearer never had a good sickle, 29

Sight: Out of sight, out of mind, 550

Silence, silent: Silence gives consent, 601; Speech is silver, silence is golden, 613; There is a time to speak and a time to be silent, 652

Silk: He that hath no silver in his purse should have silk in his tongue, 276; You cannot make a silk purse out of a sow's ear, 784

Silver: Every cloud has a silver lining, 171; He that hath not silver in his purse should have silk in his tongue, 276; Speech is silver, silence is golden, 613

Sin, sins: Charity covers a multitude of sins, 79; Poverty is no sin, 561; There is a sin of omission as well as of commission, 650

Skeleton: Every family has a skeleton in the cupboard, 174

Skill: It needs more skill than I can tell to play the second fiddle well, 371

Skittles: Life is not all beer and skittles, 403

Slave, slaves: He who goes against the fashion is himself its slave, 289; We are all slaves of opinion, 719

Slip: There's many a slip 'twixt the cup and the lip, 655

Smoke: There is no smoke without fire, 665

Snake: Take heed of the snake in the grass, 632

Soberness: What soberness conceals, drunkenness reveals, 738

Solitude: A great city, a great solitude, 254

Son: Like father, like son, 409

Sorry: Better be sure than sorry, 45

Soul: Brevity is the soul of wit, 61; Open confession is good for the soul, 544

Sow (n.): You cannot make a silk purse out of a sow's ear, 784

Sow (v.): As you sow, so shall you reap, 24; One man sows and another reaps, 534; Sow the wind and reap the whirlwind, 608; The young will sow their wild oats, 798

Spade: Call a spade a spade, 67

Speed: More haste, less speed, 470

Spirit: The spirit is willing, but the flesh is weak, 614

Spoon: He should have a long spoon that sups with the devil, 270; He who gives fair words feeds you with an empty spoon, 288

Sprat: Throw out a sprat to catch a mackerel, 684

Stable: It is too late to lock the stable when the horse has been stolen, 369

Stake: Nothing stake, nothing draw, 521

Star, stars: Hitch your wagon to a star, 307; Through hardship to the stars, 682

Steel: The tongue is not steel, yet it cuts, 694

Sticks and stones may break my bones, but words will never hurt me, 615.

Stile: Help a lame dog over a stile, 302

Stitch: A stitch in time saves nine, 619

Stomach: The way to a man's heart is through his stomach, 718

Stone, stones: Cast not the first stone, 71; Constant dripping wears away the stone, 90; A rolling stone gathers no moss, 587; Sticks and stones may break my bones, but words will never hurt me, 615; Those who live in glass houses should not throw stones, 680; Whether the pitcher strikes the stone, or the stone the pitcher, it is bad for the pitcher, 758; You cannot get blood (or water) out of a stone, 780

Stools: Between two stools you fall to the ground, 51

Storm: After a storm comes a calm, 6; Any port in a storm, 18

Straw: A drowning man will clutch at a straw, 153; The last straw breaks the camel's back, 386; A straw will show which way the wind blows, 621; You cannot make bricks without straw, 786

Stream: Cross the stream where it is shallowest, 98; Don't change horses in mid-stream, 123; It is ill striving against the stream, 362

Study: The proper study of mankind is man, 570

Sublime: From the sublime to the ridiculous is but a step, 227

Substance: Catch not at the shadow and lose the substance, 75

Success: Nothing succeeds like success, 522; Success has many friends, 626

Summer: One swallow does not make a summer, 540

Sun: If there were no clouds, we should not enjoy the sun, 328; Let not the sun go down on your wrath, 394; Light not a candle to the sun, 406; Make hay while the sun shines, 436; The sun is never the worse for shining on a dunghill, 628; There is nothing new under the sun, 668

Sundial: What is the good of a sundial in the shade?, 731
Swallow: One swallow does not make a summer, 540
Swine: Do not cast your pearls before swine, 122
Swings: What one loses on the swings one makes up on the roundabouts, 737
Sword, swords: Gluttony kills more than the sword, 238; The pen is mightier than the sword, 553; Words cut more than swords, 772

T

Tailor: The tailor makes the man, 630
Tale, tales: Dead men tell no tales, 104; Don't tell tales out of school, 148; A good tale is none the worse for being told twice, 250; A tale never loses in the telling, 640
Tar: It is no use spoiling the ship for a ha'p'orth of tar, 367
Taste, tastes: Everyone to his taste, 188; Tastes differ, 642; There is no disputing about tastes, 657
Tattler: Avoid a questioner, for he is also a tattler, 26
Teeth, *see* Tooth
Thanks: A forced kindness deserves no thanks, 221
Thief, thieves: All are not thieves that dogs bark at, 7; Give a thief enough rope and he'll hang himself, 232; Opportunity makes the thief, 545; Procrastination is the thief of time, 567; The receiver is as bad as the thief, 580; Set a thief to catch a thief, 598; There is honour among thieves, 653; When thieves fall out, honest men come by their own, 753
Thorn: There is no rose without a thorn, 663
Thought, thoughts: Second thoughts are best, 593; The wish is father to the thought, 768
Threats: Never make threats you cannot carry out, 489
Thrive: First thrive and then wive, 213
Tide: There is a tide in the affairs of men . . ., 651; Time and tide wait for no man, 685
Tiger: He who rides a tiger is afraid to dismount, 295
Time, times: Busiest men find the most time, 66; Footprints on the sands of time are not made by sitting down, 218; Life is short and time is swift, 404; Other times, other manners, 547; Procrastination is the thief of time, 567; A stitch in time saves nine, 619; Take time by the forelock, 639; There is a time to speak and a time to be silent, 652; There is no time like the present, 666; Time and tide wait for no man, 685; Time flies, 686; Time is money, 687; Time is the great healer, 688; Times change, 689; What may be done at any time is done at no time, 735; The worse luck now, the better another time, 773

Today, tomorrow: Better an egg today than a hen tomorrow, 42; Jam tomorrow and jam yesterday – but never jam today, 377; Never put off till tomorrow what may be done today, 491; Tomorrow is another day, 691; Tomorrow never comes, 692

Tongue: He cannot speak well that cannot hold his tongue, 266; He that hath not silver in his purse should have silk in his tongue, 276; A still tongue makes a wise head, 616; The tongue ever turns to the aching tooth, 693; The tongue is not steel, yet it cuts, 694

Tools: A bad workman always blames his tools, 30; Give us the tools, and we will finish the job, 237; It is ill jesting with edged tools, 361; What is a workman without his tools?, 727

Tooth, teeth: An eye for an eye, and a tooth for a tooth, 199; The gods send nuts to those who have no teeth, 243; If you cannot bite never show your teeth, 331; The tongue ever turns to the aching tooth, 693

Town: God made the country, and man made the town, 241

Trade, trades: A Jack of all trades is master of none, 376; There are tricks in every trade, 646; Two of a trade can never agree, 704

Travels: Bad news travels fast, 27; He travels the fastest who travels alone, 284

Tree, trees: Some people cannot see the wood for the trees, 607; A tree is known by its fruit, 697

Tricks: There are tricks in every trade, 646; You cannot teach an old dog new tricks, 791

Trouble, troubled: Don't meet trouble half-way, 137; It is good fishing in troubled waters, 360; Never trouble trouble till trouble troubles you, 496

Trout: You must lose a fly to catch a trout, 795

Truth: In wine there is truth, 346; A liar is not believed when he tells the truth, 401; Speak the truth and shame the devil, 611; The sting of a reproach is the truth of it, 618; Truth is stranger than fiction, 698; The truth will out, 699

Tune: He who pays the piper calls the tune, 293; There's many a good tune played on an old fiddle, 654

U

Unexpected: It is the unexpected that always happens, 368; Nothing is so certain as the unexpected, 518

United we stand, divided we fall, 707

V

Vacuum: Nature abhors a vacuum, 478

Valet: No man is a hero to his valet, 503
Valour: Discretion is the better part of valour, 117
Variety is the spice of life, 708
Venture: Nothing venture, nothing have, 523
Verb. sap., 709
Vessels: Empty vessels make the most sound, 163
Vice: Hypocrisy is a homage that vice pays to virtue, 316
View: Distance lends enchantment to the view, 118
Virtue, virtues: Every man has the defects of his own virtues, 182; Hypocrisy is a homage that vice pays to virtue, 316; Patience is a virtue, 552; Virtue is its own reward, 710
Voice: The voice of the people is the voice of God, 711
Volunteer: One volunteer is worth two pressed men, 542

W

Wag: Let the world wag, 400
Wagon: Hitch your wagon to a star, 307
Wait, waits, waiting: Everything comes to him who waits, 189; It is ill waiting for dead men's shoes, 363; They also serve who only stand and wait, 672; Time and tide wait for no man, 685
Wall, walls: The apples on the other side of the wall are the sweetest, 20; Walls have ears, 713; The weakest goes to the wall, 721
Want: Want is the mother of industry, 714; Waste not, want not, 715
War: All's fair in love and war, 10; If you want peace, prepare for war, 336; When Greek meets Greek, then comes the tug of war, 744
Waste: Haste makes waste, 264; Waste not, want not, 715
Water, waters: Blood is thicker than water, 57; Don't empty the baby out with the bath water, 130; Don't pour out the dirty water before you have clean, 139; It is good fishing in troubled waters, 360; A mill cannot grind with the water that is past, 461; Still waters run deep, 617; Water is a boon in the desert, but the drowning man curses it, 717; You cannot get water out of a stone, 780; You may lead a horse to the water, but you cannot make him drink, 793
Wealth: Health is better than wealth, 298
Wedge: The thin end of the wedge is dangerous, 674
Wedlock is a padlock, 722
Weeds: Ill weeds grow apace, 339; A man of words and not of deeds is like a garden full of weeds, 442; There is no garden without its weeds, 659
Weep: Laugh and the world laughs with you, weep and you weep alone, 388
Welcome: A constant guest is never welcome, 91; Do not wear out your welcome, 150

West: East or west, home is best, 159

Wheat: There is no wheat without chaff, 667

Wheel, wheels: Don't speak to the man at the wheel, 145; There are wheels within wheels, 648; The worst wheel of the cart creaks most, 775

Wherefore: Every why has a wherefore, 186

Whirlwind: Sow the wind and reap the whirlwind, 608

White: Two blacks do not make a white, 700

Why: Every why has a wherefore, 186

Wicked: There is no peace for the wicked, 660

Wife: A good husband makes a good wife, 248; He that hath wife and children hath given hostages to fortune, 277; Who is worse shod than the shoemaker's wife?, 761

Will: Take the will for the deed, 636; Where there's a will there's a way, 755

Win, wins: Slow but sure wins the race, 603; Win at first and lose at last, 765

Wind: God tempers the wind to the shorn lamb, 242; Hoist your sail when the wind is fair, 308; It's an ill wind that blows nobody any good, 352; It is as well to know which way the wind blows, 353; Sow the wind and reap the whirlwind, 608; A straw will show which way the wind blows, 621

Window: When the wolf comes in at the door, love creeps out of the window, 751

Wine: Do not put new wine into old bottles, 141; Good wine needs no bush, 251; In wine there is truth, 346

Wink: A nod is as good as a wink, 510; A nod is as good as a wink to a blind horse, 511

Wisdom: Experience is the mother of wisdom, 196

Wise: It is easy to be wise after the event, 358; Some are wise and some are otherwise, 606; A still tongue makes a wise head, 616; Where ignorance is bliss, 'tis folly to be wise, 754; A wise man is never less alone than when alone, 766; Wise men learn by other men's mistakes; fools by their own, 767; A word is enough to the wise, 770

Wish, wishes: The wish is father to the thought, 768; If wishes were horses, beggars would ride, 330

Wit, wits: Brevity is the soul of wit, 61; Let not your wits go wool-gathering, 396; An ounce of discretion is worth a pound of wit, 548

Wive: First thrive and then wive, 213

Wolf: A growing youth has a wolf in his belly, 257; It is a foolish sheep that makes the wolf his confessor, 348; When the wolf comes in at the door, love creeps out of the window, 751; Who keeps company with the wolf will learn to howl, 762

Woman, women: A man is as old as he feels, and a woman as old as she looks, 441; Men make houses, women make homes, 458

Wonder: A wonder lasts but nine days, 769

Wood: Do not halloo till you are out of the wood, 131; Some people cannot see the wood for the trees, 607

Word, words: Actions speak louder than words, 3; Deeds, not words, 106; Fine words butter no parsnips, 207; He who gives fair words feeds you with an empty spoon, 288; A man of words and not of deeds is like a garden full of weeds, 442; Sticks and stones may break my bones, but words will never hurt me, 615; There's many a true word spoken in jest, 656; When the word is out it belongs to another, 752; A word is enough to the wise, 770; A word spoken is past recalling, 771; Words cut more than swords, 772

Work: All work and no play makes Jack a dull boy, 17; The devil finds work for idle hands to do, 111; Many hands make light work, 447

Workman: A bad workman always blames his tools, 30; What is a workman without his tools?, 727

World: Half the world knows not how the other half lives, 259; The hand that rocks the cradle rules the world, 260; It is love that makes the world go round, 364; It takes all sorts to make a world, 373; Laugh and the world laughs with you, weep and you weep alone, 388; Let the world wag, 400; One touch of nature makes the whole world kin, 541

Worm: The early bird catches the worm, 156; Even a worm will turn, 168

Wrath: Let not the sun go down on your wrath, 394; A soft answer turneth away wrath, 605

Wrong, wrongs: Submitting to one wrong brings on another, 625; Two wrongs do not make a right, 705

Y

Yard: Give knaves an inch and they will take a yard, 235

Year, years: Christmas comes but once a year, 83; It will be all the same a hundred years hence, 375

Yesterday: Jam tomorrow and jam yesterday – but never jam today, 377

Young: Better be an old man's darling than a young man's slave, 44; Those whom the gods love die young, 681; You cannot put old heads on young shoulders, 787; The young will sow their wild oats, 798

Youth: A growing youth has a wolf in his belly, 257; Youth will be served, 799

Z

Zeal without knowledge is a runaway horse, 800